Purpose of this Book

This book is intended to be used both as an educational and training text to assist peace officers and law enforcement agencies with their response to domestic violence in the state of California. It is merely a reference and not intended to be a directive to set policy or guidelines for any law enforcement agency. This publication is <u>not</u> endorsed by the State of California, the California Commission on Peace Officer Standards and Training, or any government agency. Peace officers should always follow the law and their agency's policies and procedures when dealing with domestic violence.

DOMESTIC VIOLENCE RESPONSE
A GUIDE FOR CALIFORNIA PEACE OFFICERS

Randy E. Latham
Police Lieutenant (Ret.)

authorHOUSE®

AuthorHouse™
1663 Liberty Drive, Suite 200
Bloomington, IN 47403
www.authorhouse.com
Phone: 1-800-839-8640

This book is a work of non-fiction. Unless otherwise noted, the author and the publisher make no explicit guarantees as to the accuracy of the information contained in this book and in some cases, names of people and places have been altered to protect their privacy.

First published by AuthorHouse 8/26/2009

ISBN: 978-1-4389-5081-5 (sc)

Printed in the United States of America
Bloomington, Indiana

This book is printed on acid-free paper.

To mom:

You were always there.

Contents

ABOUT THE AUTHOR

Randy E. Latham is a retired police lieutenant from the La Verne Police Department in Los Angeles County. After many years of investigating and supervising cases of domestic violence, Randy authored the La Verne Police Department's domestic violence response course in 1999, which was certified by California POST.

Lieutenant Latham is a domestic violence response update instructor with a major southern California police academy and is on the instructor staff with a private police training consulting firm in Orange County. In addition to authoring two recent POST certified domestic violence response courses for the afore mentioned training facilities, Randy has conducted 10 years of study into laws, restraining orders and procedures related to domestic violence. Randy Latham has instructed hundreds of peace officers on the proper law enforcement response to domestic violence. He has interviewed various instructors, investigators, deputy district attorneys, commissioners and court judges with experience in dealing with domestic violence cases.

Lieutenant Latham holds an associate degree in law enforcement from Chaffey College and a bachelor's degree in management from the University of Redlands. He possesses basic through supervisory POST certificates and completed the POST management course accredited through Cal State University at Long Beach.

Randy lives in La Verne, California with his wife, Sophia.

The author can be reached via mail by writing to:

Randy E. Latham
P.O. Box 7604
La Verne, CA 91750

Or via e-mail at: dvcop@verizon.net

ACKNOWLEDGMENTS

I am a very lucky person. I was allowed to pursue a career that I absolutely loved for 33 years. Even since I officially retired from law enforcement, I have been blessed to continue being a part of this magnificent profession by assisting in training the peace officers of today.

Writing this book is a part of this blessing. Clearly there are many people who supported and greatly enhanced my professional development in various ways which in turn aided in this project. Obviously the list of those I owe a debt of gratitude far exceeds what I might be able to mention in this simple acknowledgement. That said, I would like to offer my thanks to a few of those below.

First and foremost, I want to thank Sergeant John Hampton who, nearly 40 years ago after honorably retiring from the Los Angeles Police Department, became the head of the Police Science Department at El Camino College in Torrance, California. Sergeant Hampton strived to instill the importance of meticulous preparation in those serious about entering this profession. He drilled into his students how to properly complete an application form; how to plan and dress appropriately for the oral interview; even how to walk and talk; and how to build up and present the cop's demeanor. There is no doubt this man has most certainly moved on to a much better place.

With great admiration, I wish to thank retired Lieutenant Ed Morrett. Ed was the greatest watch commander and natural leader of cops that I have ever had the honor to have known. With an almost x-ray like ability, Lieutenant Morrett could see inside people. He could immediately identify those filled with potential and those filled with bull. Ed could see the great things in others that they would never have seen in themselves. A leader, mentor, motivator and friend, Ed Morrett will always be the "cop's cop" who worried everyday about his troops in the field. I loved working for this man. God bless you Ed.

Many thanks go to my great Police Captain (now a great Chief of Police of a neighboring city) Chuck Montoya. Captain Montoya was assigned to achieve specific goals for improvement within our police department. He was a monument of decisiveness, quality judgment and production. This captain recognized capable people who really worked hard and accomplished things and held those who failed to do their job accountable. This man got the job done. Thanks for your advice, mentoring, and being an exemplar of drive and dedication. I owe you a lot.

There are many Chiefs of Police. Just a few are great, many more are good, some mediocre and a few, well, are just pretty bad. Of the Chiefs of Police that I have worked for, thanks go out to three great ones. Chief Wes Stearns was a decent hard working man who never forgot about the cops on the street. A more ethical Chief you will never find. Cops who worked for this man really didn't need a policy manual with rules outlining what would happen if they did wrong. Just the thought of disappointing this pillar of integrity would have made you want to go hang yourself. Chief Stearns had a "Father Knows Best" demeanor about him that he shared with others through osmosis. The needle of the moral compass was always pointing directly at this man.

Chief Ron Ingels brought our police department forward to a new age. By enhancing professional training, developing improvements in vehicles, weapons, technology, citizen volunteer programs and creating diversity in special assignments, Chief Ingels not only advanced officers' development but improved safety and police services to the community as well. Chief Ingels was a great leader with strong decision making capabilities.

Chief Scott Pickwith continues to deliver high quality police services to the same community that we served together for many years. Chief Pickwith is the beacon which continues to bring all members of the department together. He values individual diversity in officers and staff while simultaneously directing a team approach to accomplish the common good of proactive law enforcement goals. This Chief's administrative demeanor is one which uses the smooth approach in guiding others while quietly holding the readiness to swing the "big stick" when and where necessary to get the job done. He is a good man who cares for others . . . especially his troops.

Thanks to each of these great leaders for their service, guidance and support. Each has contributed so much to my development in the law enforcement profession.

So many thanks go to Superior Court Commissioner Jane Shade. This professor of law and former assistant head deputy supervisor of a family violence unit of a district attorney's office has been such an incredible source of assistance and inspiration to my development as a domestic violence response instructor. For 10 years, this highly motivated domestic violence response expert has provided knowledge, guidance, and critical review to my efforts in this vital arena of law enforcement training. My growth in this field would have never occurred had it not been for this great lady.

Lastly and mostly, my thanks to my wife, Sophia, for supporting me in so many ways with my goal to teach and write about the proper peace officer response to domestic violence.

INTRODUCTION

It is the hope of this author to assist individual peace officers in California with their official response to domestic violence (DV). Additionally, the intent is to assist some law enforcement agencies themselves in their response to domestic violence. Certainly, many law enforcement agencies already have up-to-date policies and procedures in place which are effectively being used everyday in dealing with this cultural and criminal phenomenon.

But, the reality is that many officers, and some agencies, are not following up-to-date peace officer response to domestic violence guidelines and laws. In some agencies, the problem of being antiquated in this field is not even realized. Sadly, in some instances, ambivalence and even laziness deepens the stigma that law enforcement simply does not care. Harsh words? Perhaps; but to deny the existence of this attitudinal reality, where it does exist, continues law enforcement's poor response to this incessantly serious problem. When this happens, law enforcement fails to protect victims of domestic violence and actually rewards the abusers. Moreover, without proper police response to this continual criminal assault upon our families, the social cloud of domestic violence thickens and blankets the very community peace officers are sworn to protect.

Law enforcement professionals must be vigilant, as agency administrators and individual officers, and drive themselves to stay on top of current laws, procedures and guidelines so as to apply the most up-to-date methods to assist victims, arrest abusers, and curb reoccurrence of domestic violence.

Perhaps one of the most vivid examples of how local law enforcement in California are not all on the same page when it comes to using up-to-date methods in curbing domestic violence, is the lack of the use of "verbal notice by a peace officer" of a restraining or protective order upon a restrained party procedure. Similar to an officer making a verbal notice to a driver that his or her drivers license is suspended, a peace officer may serve verbal notice to a restrained party that he or she has a restraining or protective order against them. Most of the law enforcement officers from other agencies I have come in contact with, tell me their departments do not use such a procedure when it comes to serving court orders.

Service or notice of the restraining or protective order is extremely important in the response to DV. No service = no arrest. The restrained party can not be prosecuted if he or she has not been served notice of the court order. A peace officer serving "verbal notice" upon a restrained party is a quick and simple method that, if carried out statewide, would dramatically increase arrests and help protect victims. After such notice, any restrained party contacting a protected party or otherwise violating the court orders, would be subject to arrest. Many times officers contact people who are determined to have such court orders against them, but the officers do not possess the "hard copies" of the orders to serve. However, since the orders are in the Domestic Violence Restraining Order System (DVROS), dispatchers can provide the specifics of the orders to the officer in the field who could then notify the restrained party.

For example, while in office, former State of California Attorney General Bill Lockyer made formal announcements regarding the fact that many thousands of court restraining orders go unserved every year. Those court orders were unenforceable due to the restrained party not being served. The many law enforcement agencies that only serve "hard copies" of court orders could serve many more orders "verbally" if they had a policy and a form (to document the specifics of the verbal notice) in place.

Many times officers respond to the call that a restrained party is at the protected party's location, only to find the restrained party was never served, thus no arrest. Throughout California, thousands of additional court orders could be served each year by peace officer verbal notice, making many thousands of additional restrained parties subject to arrest.

It is unexplainable why this great tool (verbal notice) against domestic violence is used in such a haphazard manner. Some counties (and city agencies within) use peace officer verbal notice and some do not. For example, most Orange County peace officers that I have spoken with are familiar with this verbal service of a court order method, while most Los Angeles County peace officers tell me their agency does not use verbal notice of court orders.

There is some confusion and disagreement amongst law enforcement itself about the legality of verbal notice. Some in law enforcement personally see verbal service as "not being fair" so they don't want to use that method. Some believe a peace officer can only serve an order verbally "while at the scene of domestic violence" citing PC 836 (c)(2). *However, PC 836 (c)(2) is only one authority allowing verbal notice. There are other authorities in law which allow verbal notice of a court order to be made to a restrained party which do not specifically require the officer to be at the scene of DV.* Some other authorities (some do and some do not require the officer to be at a DV scene) are Family Code Sections 6224, 6381, 6383 and 6385. Further, if the verbal notice is legal in Superior Court in Orange County, then such notice would be legal in other counties throughout California. Therefore, if an officer made a traffic stop on a driver and dispatch advised the officer the driver had an unserved restraining order against him or her, then the officer could make a proper verbal notice to the restrained party (driver) even though the traffic stop was not at the scene of domestic violence.

Verbal notice by an officer to a restrained party of a court order is explained further in this book along with a sample form and procedures for making such notice, along with updating the Domestic Violence Restraining Order System (DVROS) to then show the order "served".

Another clear example of how local law enforcement in California are not all on the same page when it comes to using up-to-date methods in curbing domestic violence, is that some agencies frequently (if not nearly always) cite release (O.R.), after booking, persons arrested for misdemeanor charges of domestic violence. This includes cite releases for violations of a restraining or protective order (PC 273.6 and PC 166) and domestic violence battery (PC 243 [e][1]). *In many cases, such releases may not be authorized as described in PC 853.6 and PC 1270.1.* Further, many such releases would not follow POST guidelines *or the recommendations by the Judicial Council of California – Final Report of the Domestic Violence Practice and Procedure Task Force – January 2008 – (specifically pages 32 & 33).* Law enforcement agencies' "risk management" should be very concerned over any such improper release of an arrested domestic violence abuser who could then make additional attacks upon the initial victim. The phrases, "had it not been for" and "knew or should have known" come to my mind when improper acts could, perhaps, lead to foreseeable and preventable attacks and injuries upon victims.

No other single factor to improve the response to domestic violence is greater than *the willingness to change!* If you believe everything is fine because "we have always done it this way" . . . then in all probability, it is not fine. If you have not updated your agency or yourself by thinking "it is not that important" . . . the reality is, it is extremely important – to the victims, the children, the abusers, the officers, the agencies and to our society.

Knowledge is great, but it is only one half of the proper police response to domestic violence. Knowledge must be consistently and effectively exercised. The finest tools in the world work only when placed in the hands of skilled craftsmen who utilize them.

We have plenty of fine tools to combat domestic violence. *Now is the time for law enforcement craftsmen to use them.*

I. POLICE RESPONSE TO DOMESTIC VIOLENCE IN CALIFORNIA

Police response to domestic violence (DV) in California is unique. Although most, if not all, states have domestic violence laws and procedures, California's laws and procedures are considered by many in the criminal justice system as some of the most comprehensive and stringent in the country.

While California's domestic violence (DV) laws have statewide authority, in practice it is clear that some counties function quite differently than others when it comes to using DV laws and procedures in a consistent and efficient manner. *The result is, on its face, that each county appears to function somewhat like its own "state" when it comes to deciding how aggressive it will pursue the DV offender.* The court, district attorney's office and local law enforcement in some counties seem to function largely by "this is the way we have always done it."

Moreover, many law enforcement agencies that handle DV incidents fail to use existing DV laws and procedures to their fullest potential. By failing to use up-to-date DV curbing "tools" consistently, law enforcement, in some cases, actually worsen the cultural and criminal phenomenon of DV. Failing to act properly or failing to act at all can have tragic results for victims of DV and, in some cases, create civil liability and citizen complaints for law enforcement.

Below are some examples of how an officer, not following California DV laws and California Commission on Peace Officer Standards and Training (POST) DV guidelines, can fail to act properly in a DV incident:

- Failure to make a mandatory arrest – *as directed by POST Guidelines.*

- Failure to attempt to obtain an emergency protective order (EPO) when a reasonable officer would believe the person requesting the order is in immediate and present danger – *as required by law.*

- Failure to properly serve a restrained party to a restraining/ protective order, when service was possible – *as required by law.*

- Failure to provide DV victims with emergency medical assistance or proper written DV victim information notices – *as required by law.*

- Failure of officers to make a mandatory arrest of a suspect for violation of a protective order and who then depart the scene leaving the DV victim with the abuser, *thus failing to protect the victim and failing to make that mandatory arrest – as required by law.*

- Failure to take a mandatory DV report or failure to take a proper DV report covering information – *as required by law.*

- Failure, while at the scene of a DV call, to seize certain deadly weapons that are in plain sight or discovered by consent – *as required by law.*

On the brighter side, some counties' agencies (courts, district attorneys and law enforcement) have taken a more proactive and progressive approach to responding to domestic violence: by using courts for DV cases which have special training and provide better victim services; by using special prosecutors from the district attorney's office who are trained and experienced in DV cases; and by having law enforcement that uses up to date DV related laws, authorities, procedures, forms and court orders to their fullest extent.

<u>And that brings us to the purpose of this training guide:</u> <u>The use of up-to-date DV related laws, authorities, procedures, forms and court orders to their fullest extent . . . by you, the law enforcement officer.</u>

It is true that you, the individual officer, can not control the courts. It is also true that you can not create victim services within the county system. And yes, it is true that you can not control what cases the district attorney chooses to file or reject.

However, you, the local law enforcement officer, can control whether or not you make a significant difference in the lives of domestic violence victims. You can help protect victims of DV. You can help protect innocent children. You can help stop DV from reoccurring. And you can help now more effectively than ever! *It only takes knowledge of the proper DV response tools and a willingness to use them.*

But first, unless you are already an officer that is actually *using* the latest DV laws and procedures to stop abusers and protect victims, *you must be willing to change.* Change by availing yourself of up-to-date DV laws and procedures. Change by using these laws and procedures (tools) whenever possible.

Like the '80s hit song said, "Get a new attitude!" Don't wait for someone else in your law enforcement agency to get the ball rolling. Unless you are confident you are being provided with the best DV training and information available, go get it yourself.

II. HOW TO START CHANGE FOR THE BETTER

<u>First, you should review the training, procedures and policies that your agency currently utilizes.</u> You may discover the procedures and policies do contain or allow, use of up-to-date DV guidelines and law. *If so, you need only use the latest laws, procedures and guidelines. This book will assist you with those efforts.*

That said, if you discover there are inadequacies in your agency's DV response procedures, do not go off half-cocked or be the "Lone Ranger". If you find that such inadequacies exist, follow whatever your agency's protocol is to update and change training, procedures and policy. Perhaps you can do some research, point to another agency's procedures that are more up to date and effective, and then forward that information to your agency's appropriate training or policy personnel, or make a presentation to the administration. *What ever it takes . . . you need to do it!*

Be prepared to point out what your agency does now to respond to DV; what the law and the California Peace Officer Standards and Training (POST) says you should be doing; and then point out how proactive agencies respond to domestic violence, using the very laws and procedures that you are proposing.

Proper police response to DV takes a team effort: your agency's administration must back the goal of using the latest DV response laws and procedures; records personnel must understand that the volume of DV reports may increase when laws and POST guidelines for documentation are followed; communication officers need proper DV training too, as they are often the first law enforcement employee contacted by victims; shift supervisors and detectives need up-to-date DV training so they understand how proper DV investigations, reporting, arrests and issuance of emergency protective orders should be pursued.

Once an agency or officer recognizes the need to improve, personnel need to be sent to proper up-to-date training classes. All officers and dispatchers receive response to domestic violence training in their basic academy or school. However, it is after that basic training when the lack of proper "continual" professional education in this area arises. *Some agencies continue on by never updating training in the proper police response to domestic violence; this in direct violation of state law – Section 13519 (g) of the California Penal Code – which mandates that officers have update training in the response to domestic violence every two years. However, it is key that supervisors and management also have such training.*

III. NOW YOU ARE READY!

Okay, you have either confirmed that you can move immediately to use current DV laws, procedures and guidelines (if your agency is up-to-date) or you have helped bring your agency up-to-date in DV training as outlined above. Either way, you are ready to take effective action. *Nothing else is holding you back . . . because now you are ready!*

You, *the cop on the street*, are the one who is going to contact the DV suspect, victim, witness and child. When you first arrive on scene . . . don't look for the judge as he or she will not be there; the prosecutor will not be present to assist you; and victim advocates are nowhere to be found. Since *you* are there to handle the situation, handle it correctly.

My fellow peace officers; you have the ability to help sufferers of domestic violence. These victims and their children turn to you for help. *While help is not easy, clean or quick, you have taken a most solemn oath to serve and protect.* You must use all legal tools and methods available to carry out that duty; for there is no one else who will.

IV. SOME COMMON PITFALLS TO AVOID

<u>"WHY SHOULD I CARE? SHE (OR HE) MUST LIKE IT!"</u> This pitfall exists in the very dynamics of DV itself. Do not give up on the victims because they are hesitant to prosecute or even if they become upset with you. DV victims have typically been repeatedly emotionally and/ or physically abused and usually over a period of time. They often feel hopeless and that somehow, it (the assault, crime, or overall abuse) is their fault. Their life has been regimented by the abuser using power and control over them to the point the victim believes there is no way out. Remember, children who are abused by a parent will often defend that same parent and/ or even deny that the abuse ever took place. Similarly, a DV victim in some cases will deny the abuse and even protect the abuser.

On the other hand, you have to care . . . if for no other reason, it's your job! Hopefully, you care for personal and professional reasons. You have a moral and legal obligation to protect life.

- <u>How to handle this</u>: follow laws, California Peace Officer Standards and Training (POST) guidelines and department policy . . . consistently. Follow these plans of action even if the victim does not want you to do so. You do what you have to do, not how the victim or suspect wants you to handle it, but rather how the law and POST guidelines direct you. Again, you should follow these plans consistently.

  o *Take all required reports of DV*

  o *Conduct complete and accurate investigations with attention paid to photos/ video, seizing evidence, recording statements by all parties (including any children involved), cover the history and other locations of the prior abuse.*

  o *Issue victim notification cards/ info handouts when required (or even when not required to assist "potential" future victims).*

  o *Make arrests as required by law.*

  o *Arrest only the dominant (aka primary) aggressor, whenever possible (although sometimes that will not be possible).*

  o *When an arrest is made, give the victim a V.I.N.E. information form/ sheet (or equivalent, if your county has such a V.I.N.E. system) as this allows the victim to be notified if the abuser is released from jail. [V.I.N.E. is a "Victim Information & Notification Everyday" automated system that allows victims to register over the telephone using a PIN number chosen by the caller/ victim. The Los Angeles County Sheriff's Department has such a system with instructions on their internet web site.*

  o *Take steps to legally prevent arrested abusers from being released on their own recognizance (O.R.).*

  o *Seek bail enhancements where appropriate.*

<u>"THE DISTRICT ATTORNEY WILL NEVER FILE THE CASE!"</u> You certainly don't have to look too far to find that pitfall. *You probably have heard that excuse (which really means "don't do your job") since you graduated from the police academy. That sounds harsh, but isn't that really the truth?* Wow! Some how, with the "district attorney" title thrown in, the phrase almost sounds like an officially condoned reason to fail to take proper police action when investigating a DV case.

After all, you (the officer) really would have done something, but, well, the "district attorney" will never file the case.

- <u>How to handle this</u>: Don't get hung up into the supposed likelihood of others (D.A., detectives, probation, court, etc.) "not doing" their job; in specific, whether a case will be filed by the prosecutor. The problem with this type of mindset is that you are pre-deciding what the district attorney is going to do with a case which in fact has not yet been reviewed by that office. Further, POST guidelines state that officers investigating a DV case should not use such reasoning to decide whether or not to make an arrest. Reality is – this is simply a fancy name to excuse being lazy.

  You (the beat officer) are to be focused on doing your job. Remember, the court, D.A., and in most cases – the detectives, are not the ones required to be the first responders to the scene of DV and to properly ACT; but YOU ARE REQUIRED TO ACT!

  In addition, there are some mandates in DV laws that require you to take certain actions. Failing to follow such mandates in the law with the excuse that you thought the "district attorney will not file the case", will not protect the victim(s) of DV; nor will that excuse provide any shield for you or your agency from possible civil liability or citizen complaint issues which may develop from failing to properly act in a DV incident.

<u>"SHE INVITED THE GUY TO COME OVER AFTER SHE HAD HIM SERVED WITH A RESTRAINING ORDER. NOW SHE CALLS US? THAT'S NOT A CRIME AND I'M NOT TAKING HIM TO JAIL".</u> Again, you certainly don't have to look far to find that pitfall. And, on its face, that logically makes sense. However, legally, it is dangerously wrong.

- <u>How to handle this</u>: While a protected party voluntarily inviting a restrained party over to visit is frustrating, restraining/ protective orders must be enforced.

  o *Except for exigent circumstances, the law requires that an officer make an arrest for a violation or a restraining/ protective order when the officer has reason to believe the person has violated the order and such person had knowledge of the order.*

  o *The terms and conditions of the protective order remain enforceable, notwithstanding the acts of the parties, and may be changed only by order of the court. In short, it doesn't matter if she let him in or not . . . the order is still valid.*

  o *Consider the consequences in a case where you, the officer, responds to a DV call: there is a DV restraining/ protective order in effect; you have knowledge of the order; the restrained party is present and has knowledge of the order (has been served) and is violating the order; there are no exigent circumstances to not make an arrest but you choose not to make the arrest because "she let him in" or even "she invited him over"; you leave and the restrained party then kills or seriously injures the protected party leaving her in a wheel chair; all this when the law required you to make an arrest where there is probable cause that a restraining/ protective order has been violated. You, the officer, simply failed to protect . . . failed to act . . . failed to obey the law.*

  Stand by for the civil lawsuit and the citizen complaint.

V. REVIEW OF BASIC DOMESTIC VIOLENCE LAWS

There are Two Types of DV Laws; (1) Authorities and (2) Crimes

DOMESTIC VIOLENCE RELATED AUTHORITIES

Relate to the legal power of the government or its agents, such as judicial officers, peace officers, etc. to act; i.e., issue or obtain a restraining order, to make an arrest, seize weapons, enhance bail, and conduct certain investigations with certain documentations. Authorities also declare legal definitions such as "domestic violence", "abuse", and "dominant aggressor", etc. DV related authorities are listed in several codes, i.e. Penal Code (PC), Family Code (FC), Code of Civil Procedure (CCP) and the Welfare and Institutions Code (W&IC).

BASIC DOMESTIC VIOLENCE ARREST & DEFINITIONS AUTHORITIES

Felony Arrest

In compliance with PC 13701, officers should make an arrest when there is probable cause that a felony offense has been committed.

Misdemeanor Arrest

- In compliance with PC 13701, officers should make an arrest when there is probable cause to believe that a misdemeanor offense has occurred in their presence.

- In compliance with PC 13701, officers shall make an arrest without a warrant whether or not the offense was committed in their presence for violations of DV protective or restraining orders.

- In compliance with PC 13701, officers shall make a lawful arrest of the person without a warrant and take that person into custody whether or not the violation occurred in the presence of the arresting officer [PC 836(c)(1)] under the following condition:

  o When a peace officer is responding to a call alleging a violation of domestic violence protective or restraining order, stalking emergency protective order, or elder abuse restraining order issued under the Family Code, Code of Civil Procedure, Welfare and Institutions Code, or the Penal Code, <u>or</u>

  o If a domestic violence protective or restraining order has been issued by the court of another state, tribe, or territory, and the peace officer has probable cause to believe that the restrained party committed an act in violation of the order, and had notice of the order and its conditions.

CA Penal Code 836 [c][3], 13519/ 13700/ 13701 – State of California Directs DV Training & Policy Requirements

- All DV training for the basic police academy and required every two-year update of DV training for officers after the academy must meet State of California (via POST) standards. This means POST must approve/ certify required training. (See PC 13519).

- The State of California determines definitions of domestic violence, abuse, dual arrest, dominant (aka primary) aggressor, officer and victim as it relates to DV laws. (See PC 836[c][3], 13700, 13701).

- The State of California requires law enforcement agencies to develop and implement written standards for officers and dispatchers response to DV. Law requires that these policies reflect that DV is alleged criminal conduct. (See PC 13701 and 13702).

  - *Policies shall encourage the arrest of DV offenders if there is probable cause that an offense has been committed.*

  - *Policies shall require the arrest of an offender, absent exigent circumstances, if there is probable cause that a protective order has been violated.*

- The State of California requires local policies that encourage arrest where there is probable cause that a DV offense has been committed (PC 13701 amended 01-01-1996). See the California Commission on Peace Officer Standards and Training (POST) web site and view their "publications list", click on "list all" and locate "Guidelines for Law Enforcement Response to Domestic Violence". Also, try the direct link to the POST DV Guidelines -

  http://www.post.ca.gov/Training/tps_bureau/domestic_violence/domestic-violence-manual_wv.pdf

  Read POST guidelines to learn there are factors that officers should not consider to avoid making a DV arrest.

CA Penal Code 13700 – Abuse and Domestic Violence – Definitions & Relationships as Related to Penal Code Crimes

- **"Abuse"** – means intentionally or recklessly causing or attempting to cause bodily injury, or placing another person in reasonable apprehension of imminent serious bodily injury to himself, herself, or another.

- **"Domestic Violence"** – means abuse committed against an adult or a minor who is a spouse, former spouse, cohabitant, former cohabitant, or person with whom the suspect has had a child, or is having or has had a dating or engagement relationship. For purposes of this document, "Cohabitant" means two unrelated adult persons living together for a substantial period of time resulting in some permanency of relationship.

  The above definition also applies to domestic violence between persons of the same gender and to any minor, emancipated or not.

  Factors to determine whether persons are cohabiting include, but are not limited to, 1) sexual relations between the parties while sharing living quarters, 2) sharing of income or expenses, 3) joint use or ownership of property, 4) whether the parties hold themselves out as husband and wife, 5) the continuity of the relationship, and 6) the length of the relationship.

CA Penal Code 13701 (b) – Dual Arrest & Dominant Aggressor - Definitions & Relationships as Related to Penal Code Crimes

- Dual Arrest - means the arrest of more than one person.

  - *Policies shall discourage, when appropriate, but not prohibit, dual arrests.*

- *Remember: Although sometimes you may have to arrest both, attempt to arrest only the dominant (aka primary) aggressor, whenever possible.*

- Dominant (aka Primary) Aggressor – means the person who is determined to be the most significant, rather than the first, aggressor.

- Officers shall make reasonable efforts to identify the dominant aggressor in any incident. In identifying the dominant aggressor, officers shall consider:

  - *The intent of the law to protect victims of DV from continuing abuse;*

  - *The threats creating fear of physical injury;*

  - *The history of DV between the persons involved; and*

  - *Whether either person acted in self-defense.*

  These above guidelines shall apply in incidents where mutual protective orders exist [PC 836(c)(3)].

- What May Happen When You Unnecessarily Arrest Both Parties – Dual Arrest

  - *You may have made the case non-prosecutable (brings doubt to a jury as to who is the real abuser).*

  - *You "re-victimized" the true victim (if there is one true victim).*

  - *You failed to protect the victim. The true victim may not call again, no matter how bad it gets!!*

  - *You taught the batterer that he or she can get away with it – by not being held accountable.*

  - *You failed to deter the violence.*

  - *You prevented the batterer from receiving counseling/ intervention, which only comes with successful prosecution.*

  - *Children may not trust the police in the future.*

  - *Children may be improperly sent to the Department of Children's Services (DCS). This may cause them to be unnecessarily traumatized.*

CA Penal Code 13701 (b) / 836 (c) (1)– Mandatory Arrest for Violation of DV Court Orders - Authorities

- Officers shall, consistent with PC 836 (c)(1) and PC 13701 (b), make a lawful arrest of the person without a warrant and take that person into custody whether or not the violation occurred in the presence of the arresting officer under the following conditions:

  - *Per 836 (c)(1) PC – When a peace officer is responding to a call alleging a violation of domestic violence protective or restraining order, stalking emergency protective order, or elder abuse restraining order.*

    1. *When the peace officer has probable cause to believe that the restrained party committed an act in violation of the order, and had notice of the order and its conditions.*

    2. *The domestic violence protective or restraining order has been issued by a court of this state, court of another state, tribe, or territory.*

  - *Per 13701 (b) PC – Policies shall require the arrest of an offender when a peace officer, absent exigent circumstances, has probable cause that a protective order has been violated (of course, to violate the order, the restrained party must have prior knowledge of its existence).*

    1. *The domestic violence protective order has been issued by a court of this state, court of another state, a commonwealth, territory, or insular possession subject to the jurisdiction of the United States, a military tribunal, or a tribe.*

CA Penal Code 836 (d) (1) – Authority to Make (Optional) Arrest for Misdemeanor Assault or Battery When DV Related

- Officers may make a warrantless arrest when there is probable cause to believe that a suspect committed an assault or battery, whether or not it has in fact been committed, upon:

  - *A current or former spouse, fiancé, fiancée;*

  - *A current or former cohabitant as defined in Section 6209 of the Family Code;*

  - *A person with whom the suspect currently is having or has previously had an engagement or dating relationship, as defined in paragraph (10) of subdivision (f) of PC 243;*

  - *A person with whom the suspect has parented a child or is presumed to have parented a child pursuant to the Uniform Parentage Act (Part 3, commencing with Section 7600 of Division 12 of the Family Code);*

  - *A child of the suspect, a child whose parentage by the suspect is the subject of an action under the Uniform Parentage Act, a child of a person in one of the above categories;*

  - *Any other person related to the suspect by consanguinity or affinity within the second degree; or*

  - *Any person who is 65 years of age or older and who is related to the suspect by blood or legal guardianship;*

- *AND– The arrest is made as soon as probable cause arises to believe that the person to be arrested has committed the assault or battery, whether or not it has in fact been committed.*

CA PENAL CODE 12028.5 – AUTHORITY TO SEIZE CERTAIN WEAPONS AT DV SCENES – SEE PENAL CODE FOR SPECIFICS

- **"Domestic Violence"** – as defined in Penal Code 12028.5 (for weapons seizure) includes the same relations & conduct as described above. Additionally domestic violence relationships for weapons seizure also includes: a child of a party or a child who is the subject of an action under the Uniform Parentage Act; a cohabitant or former cohabitant, as defined in Section 6209 of the Family Code; and any other person related by consanguinity or affinity within the second degree.

- **"Abuse"** – as defined in Penal Code 12028.5 (for weapons seizure) means to intentionally or recklessly cause or attempt to cause bodily injury; place a person in reasonable apprehension of imminent serious bodily injury to that person or to another; also includes sexual assault, to molest, attack, strike, stalk, destroy personal property; or violate terms of a DV protection order.

CA PENAL CODE 12028.5 - SYNOPSIS

- A peace officer who is at the scene of a DV incident involving a threat to human life or a physical assault, shall take temporary custody of any firearm or other deadly weapon in plain sight or discovered pursuant to a consensual or other lawful search as necessary for the protection of the peace officer or other persons present. The officer shall issue a receipt for the firearm or weapon. This seizure authority applies to:

  - *Any firearm*

  - *Any weapon, the possession or concealed carrying of which is prohibited by Section 12020 PC.*

- Section 12028.5 PC has certain conditions, requirements and restrictions affecting when and how such seized weapons are released. See actual Penal Code Section for details.

- Section 12028.5 PC states the law enforcement agency, or the individual law enforcement officer, shall not be liable for any act in the good faith exercise of this section.

CITIZEN'S (PRIVATE PERSON'S) ARREST – GOOD FAITH EFFORT TO INFORM VICTIM OF RIGHT TO MAKE A CITIZEN'S ARREST

- Any time a peace officer is called out on a domestic violence incident, it shall be mandatory that the officer make a good faith effort to inform the victim of his or her right to make a citizen's (private person) arrest. This information shall include advising the victim how to safely execute the arrest [PC 836(b)].

- Laws use to require officers to accept certain citizen's arrests and if they refused they committed a felony. Officers are no longer required (amended PC 142 and 837) to accept a private person's arrest if made pursuant to PC 837.

- Per PC 847 (b), there shall be no civil liability on the part of, and no cause of action shall arise against, any peace officer or law enforcement officer acting within the scope of his or authority, for false arrest or false imprisonment arising out of any arrest under any of the following circumstances: (1) the arrest was lawful, or the peace officer, at the time of the arrest, had reasonable cause to believe the arrest was lawful; (2) the arrest was made pursuant to a charge made, upon reasonable cause, of the commission of a felony by the person to be arrested; (3) the arrest was made pursuant to the requirements of

PC Sections *142*, *837*, 838, or 839. Note: Follow Your Agency's Policy Regarding Private Persons Arrests.

- With mandatory and optional arrest powers of peace officers, it is rarely necessary for a DV victim to make a private person's arrest. Officers will almost always be able to make the arrest under PC 836 (c), 836 (d) and 13701, in addition to standard arrest authorities.

DOMESTIC VIOLENCE RELATED CRIMES

Relate to criminal acts to which persons may be arrested and prosecuted. DV crimes are in the California Penal Code (PC).

FELONY CRIMES

CA Penal Code 273.5 (a) – Willful Infliction of Corporal Injury:

- *The Main DV Related Felony Crime*

- *Felony Arrest*

- Any person who willfully inflicts upon a person who is his or her spouse, former spouse, cohabitant, former cohabitant, or the mother or father of his or her child, corporal injury resulting in a traumatic condition, is guilty of a felony, and upon conviction thereof shall be punished by imprisonment in the state prison for two, three or four years, or in the county jail for not more than one year, or by a fine, or by both fine and imprisonment. Penalties enhanced by prior convictions of certain crimes, see Penal Code Section 273.5 (a) for details.

  - *"Traumatic Condition" – means a condition of the body, such as a wound or external or internal injury, whether of a minor or serious nature, caused by physical force.*

  - *Officers should make an arrest when there is probable cause to believe that this felony has been committed. Specifics related to this charge are:*

    1. *A DV relationship exists between the abuser and victim; and*

    2. *Corporal injury caused a traumatic condition.*

CA Penal Code 166(c)(4) – Felony Violation of a Criminal Protective or Restraining Order:

- *Felony Arrest – Special Elements*

- Second or subsequent conviction for violation of criminal protective or stay away order involving domestic violence occurring within seven years of a prior conviction for violation of any of those orders and involving an act of violence or credible threat of violence as described in (c) or (d) of 139 PC.

CA Penal Code 273.6 (d) – Felony Violation of a Protective or Restraining Order:

- *Felony Arrest – Special Elements*

- As defined in the Family Code (EPOs, TROs, Family Court), the Code of Civil Procedure (Civil Harassment Orders, Civil Court), or 15657.03 of the Welfare & Institutions Code (Elder or Dependent Adult Abuse, Civil Court) – Special crime element – A subsequent conviction for violation of an order described in 273.6 (a) PC (violation of the above court orders, first time being a misdemeanor), occurring within seven years of a prior conviction and involving an act of violence or credible threat of violence as defined in (c) of 139 PC.

CA Penal Code 273.6 (e) – Felony Violation of a Protective or Restraining Order:

- *Felony Arrest – Special Elements*

- As defined in the Family Code (EPOs, TROs, Family Court), the Code of Civil Procedure (Civil Harassment Orders, Civil Court), or 15657.03 of the Welfare & Institutions Code (Elder or Dependent Adult Abuse, Civil Court) – Special crime element – A subsequent conviction for violation of an order described in 273.6 (a) PC (violation of the above court orders, first time being a misdemeanor), occurring within one year of a prior conviction that results in physical injury to a victim.

CA Penal Code 422 – Felony Criminal Threats:

- *Felony Arrest – Special Elements*

- Any person who willfully threatens to commit a crime which will result in death or great bodily injury to another person, with the specific intent that the statement, made verbally, in writing, or by means of an electronic communication device, is to be taken as a threat, even if there is no intent of actually carrying it out, which, on its face and under the circumstances in which it is made, is so unequivocal, unconditional, immediate, and specific as to convey to the person threatened, a gravity of purpose and an immediate prospect of execution of the threat, and thereby causes that person reasonably to be in sustained fear for his or her own safety or for his or her immediate family's safety, shall be punished by imprisonment in the county jail not to exceed one year, or by imprisonment in the state prison.

- Is a *"conditional threat"* a violation of 422 PC? What is a conditional threat?

  - *A conditional threat is when a condition has been placed on carrying out the act or threat. It usually starts with, "If you . . ." i.e., "If you try to leave . . . I will kill you", "If you call the police . . . I will stab your mother" or "If you don't come home now . . . I will break your arm".*

  - *Law looks at whether words were conveyed with gravity of purpose (was the suspect serious).*

  - *Was there an immediate prospect of execution?*

  - *In the past, some courts have disagreed with each other on whether or not a conditional threat can be a violation of PC 422. However, the California Supreme Court has ruled that conditional threats are true threats and thus can violate PC 422.*

- Additional Info & Recommendations re: PC 422

  - *If the elements are there, charge and let D.A. decide.*

  - *Other similar felony charges to consider depending on the circumstances of the case being investigated – P.C. 136.1 (b)(1) or P.C. 140(a) – (Threats or intimidation of a witness).*

  - *Threats made through a third party can violate PC 422.*

- What constitutes a PC 422 criminal threat?

  - *A threat to commit a crime which if committed would result in death or great bodily injury to another person. One threat is sufficient but it must be one of death or GBI.*

  - *A threat made with specific intent that the statement be taken as a threat. It does not require that the suspect had the intent to carry out the threat. Criminal threats can be made from jail.*

  - *Remember: This type of felony serious threat must be:*

    1. *Made with the intent to place recipient in fear for self or family.*
    2. *Conveyed to the threatened person with gravity and purpose of immediate prospect of execution.*
    3. *Verbal or written or electronically communicated (such as by phones, pagers, computers, faxes, video recorders).*

CA Penal Code 646.9(b) – Felony Stalking While a Protective/ Restraining Order Prohibiting Stalking is in Place:

- *Felony Arrest – Special Elements*

- Any person who violates stalking law PC 646.9 (a)[see below] while there is a protective or restraining order in effect prohibiting the behavior described in that stalking subdivision (a) against the same party, is guilty of a *straight felony* with 2, 3 or 4 years in prison.

  - *This special stalking crime (stalking while prohibited by a restraining order) has a greater penalty than the regular stalking section of PC 646.9 (a).*

CA Penal Code 646.9(a) – Felony Stalking:

- *Felony Arrest – Special Elements*

- Any person who willfully, maliciously, and repeatedly follows or willfully and maliciously harasses another person and who makes a credible threat with intent to place that person in reasonable fear for his or her safety, or the safety of his or her immediate family is guilty of stalking.

"Harasses" – Means engaging in knowing and willful *course of conduct* directed at a specific person that seriously alarms, annoys, torments, or terrorizes the person, and that serves no legitimate purpose.

"Course of Conduct" – Means two or more acts occurring over a period of time, however short, evidencing a continuity of purpose. Constitutionally protected activity is not included with this meaning of course of conduct.

"Credible Threat" – Means a verbal or written threat, including that performed through the use of an electronic communication device, or a threat implied by a pattern of conduct or combination of verbal, written, or electronically communicated statements and conduct, made with the intent to place the person that is the target of the threat in reasonable fear for his or her safety or the safety of his or her family, and made with the apparent ability to carry out the threat.

  - *It is not necessary to prove that the defendant had the intent to actually carry out the threat. Remember: unlike PC 422, the credible threat in PC 646.9 may include a threat implied by a pattern of conduct. See code and case law for details.*

- *The present incarceration of the person making the threat shall not bar prosecution under this section.*

- *Electronic communication device includes, but is not limited to, telephones, cellular phones, computers, video recorders, fax machines, or pagers.*

- *See PC 646(a) for specifics and definition of "immediate family".*

CA Penal Code 243(d) – Felony Battery:

- *Felony Arrest*

- Battery committed against any person and serious bodily injury is inflicted on the person, the battery is punishable by imprisonment in the county jail not exceeding one year or imprisonment in state prison. Note: this is often an overlooked crime section to charge.

  - *See PC 243(f) for definition of "serious bodily injury".*

DV Related Felony Crimes – Special Note:

- Many felony crimes could be DV related. *Document as DV & arrest as such when DV circumstances/ relationships exist and the act is meant to harm, terrorize, threaten or harass the victim -* Example – PC 187, 203, 207, 236-237, 245, 246, 261-262, 368, 459, 597 – There are others!

- *Remember –"Domestic Violence Related" offenses have 2 parts: the ACT (crime) and the RELATIONSHIP of the defendant to the victim. "X" mark report as DV related (or use your agency's DV crime/ arrest report form).*

MISDEMEANOR CRIMES

CA Penal Code 243(e)(1) – Domestic Violence Battery:

- *The Main DV Related Misdemeanor Crime*

- *Misdemeanor Arrest*

- When battery is committed against a spouse, a person with whom the defendant is cohabiting, a person who is the parent of the defendant's child, former, spouse, fiancé, or fiancée, or a person with whom the defendant currently has, or has previously had, a dating or engagement relationship, the battery is punishable by a fine, or by imprisonment in a county jail for a period of not more than one year, or by both that fine and imprisonment.

CA Penal Code 273.6 (a) – Misdemeanor Violation of a Protective Order:

- *Misdemeanor Arrest*

- Any intentional and knowing violation of a protective order, as defined in Section 6218 of the Family Code (EPOs, TROs, Family Court), or of an order issued pursuant to Section 527.6 / 527.8 of the Code of Civil Procedure (Civil Harassment Orders, Civil Court), or 15657.03 Welfare & Institutions Code (Elder or Dependent Adult Abuse, Civil Court) is a misdemeanor punishable by a fine or not more that one thousand dollars, or by imprisonment in a county jail for not more than one year, or by both that fine and imprisonment – Also applies to such orders issued by a tribunal of another state (as defined by Family Code Section 6401).

CA Penal Code 166 (a)(4) – Misdemeanor Violation of a Court Order:

- *Misdemeanor Arrest*

- Willful disobedience of the terms as written of any process or court order or out-of-state court order, lawfully issued by any court, including orders pending trial – If DV related, fine is enhanced along with imprisonment in county jail – Each DV related contact with the protected person is a separate violation of the order of the court – Present incarceration of the person who makes contact with the victim is not a defense to a violation.

- Although PC 166 (a)(4) covers any court order, often DV criminal court orders are prosecuted under PC 166 (a) (4) and DV family court orders are prosecuted under PC 273.6 (a), above.

- Use PC 273.6 (a) whenever possible. It is more specific to DV violations and a conviction under PC 273.6 (a), prohibits a person in the future from possessing a firearm.

  o *PC 12021(c)(1) - Felony to possess a firearm if convicted of certain misdemeanors. Includes: PC – 136.1, 136.5, 140, 240, 241, 242, 243, 245, 246, 246.3, 273.5, 273.6, 417, 422 (plus others) - (NOTE PC 166 is not there - Charge PC 273.6 when possible).*

DV Related Misdemeanor Crimes – Special Note:

- Many misdemeanor crimes could be DV related. *Document as DV & arrest as such when DV circumstances/ relationships exist and the act is meant to harm, terrorize, threaten or harass the victim -* Example – PC 240, 417, 484, 591.5, 594, 596, 602, 602.5, 12024 – There are others!

- Remember – *"Domestic Violence Related"* offenses have 2 parts: the *ACT* (crime) and the *RELATIONSHIP* of the defendant to the victim. "X" mark report as DV related (or use your agency's DV crime/ arrest report form).

OTHER CRIMES THAT MAY BE RELATED TO A DV CRIMINAL ARREST

CA Penal Code 368(b)(1) – Elder or Dependent Adult Abuse:

- Inflicting unjustifiable physical pain or mental suffering, on any elder adult (65 years of age or older) or on any dependent adult (18 to 65 years of age) under circumstances or conditions likely to produce great bodily harm or death is guilty of a misdemeanor or felony crime, depending upon circumstances of the case. See Penal Code for details and definitions. DV could be against such an elder or dependent adult.

CA Penal Code 273a(a) & (b) – Child Abuse/ Endangering:

- Any person who, under circumstances or conditions likely to produce great bodily harm or death, willfully causes or permits any child to suffer, or inflicts thereon unjustifiable physical pain or mental suffering, or having the care or custody of any child, willfully causes or permits the person or health of that child to be injured, or willfully causes or permits that child to be placed in a situation where his or her person or health is endangered, is guilty of a misdemeanor or felony crime, depending upon circumstances of the case. See Penal Code for details and definitions. DV against another adult could create circumstances that could cause such a child abuse/ endangering crime against a child present during that DV abuse (i.e. dad stabs mother in front of 6 year old daughter = mental suffering).

The Above Crimes are Often Overlooked During DV Investigations:

- The elderly and children are often directly or indirectly abused during DV between two other people. Avoid "tunnel vision" during your DV investigations and determine if elderly and/ or children are victims of abuse or neglect. They may not even be the primary targets of the DV abuser, but they may be victims of abuse never the less. DV abusers not only abuse their direct partners, but also other people (and even pets) in the home.

VI. COURT ORDERS

TYPES OF COURT ORDERS

Criminal Restraining and Protective Orders

- PC 136.2 – Authority for court to issue.

- PC 166(a)(4) – Misdemeanor violation.

- PC 166 (c)(4)- Felony violation.

- Restrained party must have knowledge/ notice of the court order to be arrested/ prosecuted.

- Reminder – The "protected party" can not be arrested for violating the restraining/ protective order. Only the "restrained party" can violate the court order.

Family Court Restraining & Protective Orders & Emergency Protective Orders (EPOs)

- FC 6240 – 6275 – Authority for court to issue orders, definitions, service, etc.

- PC 273.6(a) – Misdemeanor violation.

- PC 273.6 (d) - Felony violation.

- PC 273.6 (e) – Felony violation.

- Restrained party must have knowledge/ notice of the court order to be arrested/ prosecuted.

- Reminder – The "protected party" can not be arrested for violating the restraining/ protective order. Only the "restrained party" can violate the court order.

Civil Court Harassment & Restraining Orders

- Code of Civil Procedure (CCP) 527.6 & 527.8 – Authority for court to issue orders, definitions, service, etc.

- PC 273.6(a) – Misdemeanor violation.

- PC 273.6 (d) - Felony violation.

- PC 273.6 (e) – Felony violation.

- Restrained party must have knowledge/ notice of the court order to be arrested/ prosecuted.

- Reminder – The "protected party" can not be arrested for violating the restraining/ protective order. Only the "restrained party" can violate the court order.

Civil Court Harassment & Restraining Orders for Elder or Dependant Adult Abuse

- 15657.03 Welfare & Institutions Code Elder or Dependent Adult Abuse – Authority for court to issue orders, definitions, service, etc.

- PC 273.6(a) – Misdemeanor violation.

- PC 273.6 (d) - Felony violation.

- PC 273.6 (e) – Felony violation.

- Restrained party must have knowledge/ notice of the court order to be arrested/ prosecuted.

- Reminder – The "protected party" can not be arrested for violating the restraining/ protective order. Only the "restrained party" can violate the court order.

Out of State Restraining and Protective Orders

- You go to a DV call where a protected party shows you an out of state DV protective/ restraining order. The order appears valid on its face; the restrained party is present; and there is proof of service (knowledge) upon the restrained party. *Can this "out of state" protective order be enforced and the restrained party be arrested? Yes!*

- Congress enacted the Violence Against Women Act (VAWA) in 1994. This act directs all jurisdictions (States, District of Columbia, Federal Territories, Possessions and Tribal Courts) to give full faith and credit to valid court orders of protection related to domestic or family violence issued by other jurisdictions (18 U.S.C. 2265)

- What evidence of the out of state order does the officer need to arrest for the violation of that order?

  - *The officer is shown a copy of the order that appears valid on its face,* **or**

  - *The law enforcement agency has a copy of the order on file,* **or**

  - *The order is filed with the Department of Justice (DOJ) Domestic Violence Restraining Order System (DVROS) CLETS computer – usually in the dispatch area. Most orders will be in the DVROS system.*

- Other requirements must be met as with any protective order violation:

  - *The restrained party has notice of the order,* **and**

  - *The restrained party violated the conditions of the order.*

  - *See (*) "Notice/ Service of Order to Restrained Party Required for Arrest & Prosecution" section below.*

- Authorities and Charges:

  - *Authorities – Title 18 U.S.C. 2265, PC 836 (c)(1), FC 6380, 6380.5, 6381.*

  - *Charges – PC 166 or PC 273.6 depending if the order is a family court or criminal court order. If in doubt, charge PC 166.*

- Get the Free Guide – "Protecting Victims of Domestic Violence – A Law Enforcement Officer's Guide to Enforcing Orders of Protection Nationwide":

  o *Distributed by the International Association of Chiefs of Police & the United States D.O.J.*

  o *Go on-line and enter the following address and open it up: http://www.theiacp.org/documents/pdfs/Publications/ACF3068.pdf – The approximate 15 page, in color, booklet will appear and you can print it out.*

OBTAINING AN EMERGENCY PROTECTIVE ORDER (EPO)

- A peace officer may request an EPO from the on-call judicial officer when there are reasonable grounds to believe:

  o *A person is in immediate and present danger of domestic violence;*

  o *A child is in immediate and present danger of abuse by a family or household member;*

  o *A child is in immediate and present danger of being abducted by a parent or relative;*

  o *A person is in immediate and present danger of stalking; or*

  o *An elder person or dependant adult is in immediate and present danger of abuse as defined in Section 15610.07 of the W&IC Code (other than solely on an allegation of financial abuse).*

- *Remember:* The domestic violence relationships defined for criminal purposes are in Penal Code Section 13700. *However, the definition of domestic violence relationships for obtaining an EPO is greatly broadened.* They include the relationships as defined in PC Section 13700 **and** those defined in Family Code Section 6211 (also see related FC 6203, 6205, 6209, 6210) which are:

  o *Spouse or former spouse.*

  o *A cohabitant or former cohabitant, as defined in FC 6209 (any person who regularly resides in the household or who formerly regularly resided in the household). This definition of "cohabitant" is much broader than that listed in PC 13700.*

  o *A person with whom the respondent is having or has had a dating or engagement relationship.*

  o *A person with whom the respondent has had a child or where there is a legal presumption that the male parent is the father of the child of the female parent under the Uniform Parentage Act.*

  o *Any other person related by consanguinity (by blood) or affinity (by marriage) within the second degree.*

- Officers should make a request for an EPO based on a person's allegation of a recent incident of abuse or threat of abuse; or when an officer has reasonable grounds to believe that a person is in immediate and present danger of stalking.

- Officers at a situation in which an officer would believe there may be grounds for an EPO *shall* inform the person for whom an EPO may be sought (or if that person is a minor, his or her parent or guardian, if they are not the potentially restrained party) that he or she may request the officer to request an EPO (FC 6275).

- An officer *shall* request an EPO if the officer believes that the person requesting the order is in immediate and present danger.

- In some cases, the victim may not want an EPO, however, a peace officer may have reason to believe the victim or child present may be in danger by the abuser. *The officer may request an EPO if the otherwise legal requirements are met, whether or not the victim request such an order.*

  - *In fact, there are no requirements in the Family Code indicating that only the victim may request an EPO. Family Code Sections 6250 - 6275 only require a peace officer to assert reasonable grounds for issuance of such an order.*

- A peace officer may request the order whether or not the abuser is at the location or is in custody.

- The fact that the endangered person has left the household to avoid abuse does not affect the availability of an EPO.

- When a judicial officer issues an order, the peace officer shall reduce the order to writing using a State of California Judicial Council approved form.

- A peace officer shall serve a copy of the order on the restrained party (if he or she can be located) and give a copy to the protected party.

- Once the EPO has been issued (and served when possible) the officer should return the order to assigned department personnel (usually dispatchers or other support staff) ASAP so that the order (along with information regarding service) can be entered into the DVROS system.

PRECEDENCE OF COURT ORDERS

Which Order to Enforce in Case of Multiple Orders

- If there is more than one civil order regarding the same parties, the officer shall enforce the order issued last. If there are both civil (includes family court) and criminal orders regarding the same parties, the officer shall enforce the criminal order issued last. See exception for EPO's below.

- Subject to the provisions below - An Emergency Protective Order (EPO) – issued by any court shall take precedence over any other restraining /protective order when . . .

  - *The EPO is to protect one or more individuals who are already protected persons under another restraining or protective order.*

  - *The EPO restrains the individual who is the restrained person in the other restraining or protective order mentioned above.*

  - *An EPO that meets these requirements shall have precedence in enforcement over the provisions of any other restraining or protective order **only with respect** to those provisions of the EPO that are more restrictive in relation to the restrained person.*

o   *See PC 136.2 (c) & FC 6383 (h).*

NOTICE/ SERVICE OF ORDER TO RESTRAINED PARTY REQUIRED FOR ARREST & PROSECUTION

Various Methods to Serve Notice of Order upon Restrained Party

- Restrained party must have prior knowledge of the court order to be arrested/ prosecuted for violation of the court order. *Any one* of the following methods shows valid knowledge/ service of the court order on the restrained party:

  o   *The order indicates the restrained party was present in court when the order was issued - FC 6380(c), 6385(b) – PC 836(c)(2).*

  o   *There is proof of personal service by a process server, other person or peace officer on file with the order at the police agency or court, listed in the DVROS or is shown to the officer. FC 6271(a), 6380(d), 6383(a), 6385(b) - PC 836(c)(2).*

  o   *The restrained party (*) has been verbally advised by a peace officer of the contents of the order. FC 6224, 6381(c), 6383(e)(f)(g), 6385(b) - PC 836(c)(2).*

Additional Information Regarding (*) Verbal Notice by a Peace Officer to Restrained Party

- *Your Agency Should Have a Policy and a One Page Check Off Form to Handle This Issue.*

- Peace officer reads a valid restraining order *or* obtains valid restraining order information from a dispatcher who is reading directly from a valid order *or* is obtaining the restraining order information from the hit in the Domestic Violence Restraining Order System (DVROS). Information must be in detail.

- Peace officer makes a verbal notice to the restrained party that he or she has a valid restraining order against them. The officer advises the restrained party of the specific contents of the order.

  o   *The restrained party will only be held accountable to the restraining order's* **specifics** *that he or she is actually told.*

  o   *All necessary information can be obtained directly from a valid order* **or** *from the dispatcher's advisement gleaned from the DVROS hit.*

  o   *The advisement should cover specifics, i.e.*

    1. *Who is the restrained party.*
    2. *Who is the protected party.*
    3. *Persons and places the restrained party must stay away from, and how far, distances, etc.*
    4. *Type of activity or conduct that is prohibited.*
    5. *Custody of minor children, with specifics (if involved).*
    6. *Firearms restrictions with specifics.*
    7. *Court name, judge name, case number, expiration date and times.*

8. Any other important specifics.

- It is strongly recommended that the officer reduce the advisement to writing by using a police department standardized "check-off" form which identifies the restrained party and documents in detail what the party was told. Remember, this is a "verbal notice" and it is not required to give the restrained party a copy of the verbal notice document at the scene. The officer signs the form and files the documented advisement as a report (with report/DR number) with his/ her department ASAP. This short one page check off report is necessary as it is retrievable documentation that the restrained party was properly verbally served with the contents of the order.

  o *The officer may request the restrained party to sign the form when completed; however, there is no law which requires the restrained party to sign such form. If that party refuses to sign, the officer should simply note "refused" on the restrained party's signature line.*

  o *Note: see sample "Verbal Notice of Restraining Order" later in this book.*

- Dispatch – Should receive the above "verbal notice by a peace officer" report directly from the issuing officer. Dispatch should immediately update the DVROS system to indicate the restraining/ protective order has now been served "verbally by a peace officer". See CLETS manual for details.

- It is *strongly recommended* that a copy of the completed "verbal notice by a peace officer" report, along with a print out of the updated DVROS hit (now showing notice served verbally by a peace officer) be faxed or mailed to the agency/ court which originally entered the unserved restraining/ protective order into the DVROS system.

- The completed "verbal notice by a peace officer" report, along with a print out of the updated DVROS hit now showing notice served verbally by a peace officer, and information that the DVROS entry agency was sent a copy, is now a completed report and is filed as any other police report would be.

FIREARMS CRIMES/ RESTRICTIONS RELATED TO DV AND/ OR RESTRAINING/ PROTECTIVE ORDERS

Prior Felony & Certain Misdemeanor Convictions Prohibit a Person from Possessing/ Controlling a Firearm and a Subsequent Violation May Result in a Felony Arrest – Check Records of Suspected DV Abusers

- **Prior Felony Conviction – PC 12021 (a) (1)** – Any person who has been convicted of a felony under the laws of the United States, the State of California, or any other state, government, or country of an offense enumerated in subdivision (a), (b), or (d) of Section 12001.6, or who is addicted to the use of any narcotic drug, and *who owns, purchases, receives, or has in his or her possession or under his or her custody or control any firearm is guilty of a felony.*

  o *Felony Arrest*

- **Prior Misdemeanor Conviction of Certain Crimes – PC 12021 (c) (1)** – Any person who has been convicted of a misdemeanor violation of Section 71, 76, 136.1, 136.5, or 140, subdivision (d) of Section 148, Section 171b, 171c, 171d, 186.28, 240, 241, 242, 243, 244.5, 245, 245.5, 246.3, 247, **273.5, 273.6,** 417, 417.6, 422, 626.9, **646.9,** 12023, or 12024, subdivision (b) or (d) of Section 12034, Section 12040, subdivision (b) of Section 12072, subdivision (a) of former Section 12100, Section 12220,

12320, or 12590, or Section 8100, 8101, or 8103 of the Welfare and Institutions Code, any firearm-related offense pursuant to Sections 871.5 and 1001.5 of the Welfare and Institutions Code, or of the conduct punished in paragraph (3) of subdivision (g) of Section 12072, and *who, within 10 years of the conviction, owns, purchases, receives, or has in his or her possession or under his or her custody or control, any firearm is guilty of an offense, punishable by imprisonment in a county jail or in the state prison.*

(See Penal Code for details. NOTE PC 166 is not there - Charge PC 273.6 when possible).

o   *Felony Arrest*

Restrained Party to a Temporary Restraining Order or Injunction who Purchases, Receives or Attempts to Purchase of Receive a Firearm

- **Felony Arrest PC 12021(g)(1)** – If the restrained party purchases, receives or attempts to purchase or receive a firearm knowing that he or she is prohibited from doing so by a temporary restraining order or injunction issued by 527.6 or 527.8 of the Code of Civil Procedure, a protective order as defined by 6218 FC, a protective order issued by 136.2 or 646.91 of the Penal Code or a protective order issued by 15657.03 of the W&IC Code, *then he or she is guilty of a public offense, which shall be punishable by imprisonment in a county jail or in the state prison.*

    o   *This is for firearms acquired after orders are served.*

    o   *Firearm prohibition warning must be printed on order to charge this offense.*

Restrained Party to a Temporary Restraining Order or Injunction who Owns or Possesses a Firearm

- **Misdemeanor Arrest PC 12021(g)(2)** – If the restrained party owns or possesses a firearm knowing that he or she is prohibited from doing so by a temporary restraining order or injunction issued by 527.6 or 527.8 of the Code of Civil Procedure, a protective order as defined by 6218 FC, a protective order issued by 136.2 or 646.91 of the Penal Code or a protective order issued by 15657.03 of the W&IC Code is guilty of a public offense, then he or she shall be punishable by imprisonment in a county jail not exceeding one year.

    o   *This is for firearms previously owned by the restrained party or otherwise possessed.*

    o   *Firearm prohibition warning must be printed on order to charge this offense.*

Failure to Relinquish a Firearm When Ordered by the Court on a Restraining/ Protective Order – Criminal Violations

- Restraining & protective orders - civil, criminal, including EPOs – may contain wording / orders for the restrained party to (1) relinquish any firearms subject to the party's immediate possession or control AND (2) file a receipt with the court showing the firearm was surrendered or sold as ordered.

o   *Check wording of orders carefully. Older orders may indicate the party has 24 hours to surrender the firearm to police (or sell it to a licensed gun dealer) and another 72 hours afterwards to file a receipt with the court.*

o   *More recent orders may indicate the party shall immediately surrender the firearm to police if requested by an officer, and if not requested the relinquishment (or selling of the gun to a licensed gun dealer) shall occur within 24 hours and a receipt filed with the court within 48 hours of the party being served.*

o   *Officers, dispatchers & property officers shall carefully read, communicate, transmit & follow the specific wording contained in court orders related to relinquishment, possession or control of firearms. Specific wording on the court order dictates what, if any, charges may apply.*

o   *Failure of the restrained party to <u>(1)</u> relinquish a firearm <u>or</u> <u>(2)</u> file a receipt with the court as ordered shall constitute a violation of the court order. For a criminal court order, the charge would be PC 166; for a civil court order (including EPOs), the charge would be PC 273.6.*

o   *Remember – In addition to a possible criminal violation of a court order for failure of the restrained party to relinquish a firearm or file a receipt with the court as ordered, if the restrained party purchases, receives, owns or possesses (including attempts) a firearm after he or she is served with a copy of the order containing firearm restrictions, he or she would be in violation of 12021 (g)(1) or (g)(2).*

VII. SUCCESSFUL ARREST & PROSECUTION & RELEASE RESTRICTIONS

PREPARE YOURSELF FOR DOMESTIC VIOLENCE INCIDENTS

Get a New Attitude!

- Re-evaluate your officer safety attitude and training. Do not become complacent when responding to DV calls. You will respond to hundreds of such calls in your career. It is easy (because you have gone to so many incidents and walked away afterwards) to become lazy and let your guard down. *DON'T DO IT! You can't help anyone if you are dead!*

- Care about DV victims, even if they don't seem to care about themselves.

- Give special concern for the safety of any children related to the incident. *In some cases, you may be the only person who cares!*

- Learn on your own; research the Penal Code, Family Code, Government Code, Welfare & Institutions Code, and case law related to DV.

- Talk with *trained & seasoned* DV investigators, Deputy D.A.'s, judges, and DV counselors. Seek out suggestions for report writing and investigations.

- Attend and complete DV update and advanced POST training classes.

- Research and help update policy and procedures in your department and follow your departments' standards for making suggestions and recommendations.

ARREST

Follow the Law & POST Guidelines

- Take mandatory DV reports.

- Make mandatory arrests for violations of restraining/ protective orders.

- Make other DV related arrests in a pro-active manner following guidelines in PC 13701 (b), "policies shall encourage the arrest of DV offenders if there is probable cause that an offense has been committed."

- Obtain an EPO when ever possible. Remember: Follow the law re: telling a DV victim of the right to request an EPO (FC 6275).

- Serve restrained parties with court orders whenever possible. *This includes making special efforts to serve such orders verbally by a peace officer whenever possible.* Such notice will require proper documentation.

- Give victims proper DV victim forms/ cards containing appropriate victim information, services and resources. This includes a V.I.N.E. form when an arrest is made, if your county has such a program (which allows a victim to register over the telephone and then be notified when the abuser is released from jail).

- Protect victims of certain crimes identity when confidentiality laws permit. *Have victim complete the appropriate confidentiality form.* See PC 293 & Government Code 6254 (f) (2) (3).

- Conduct a complete and accurate investigation and report with attention to details, getting statements (taped when possible) by all parties involved (including children when possible), seizing relevant evidence, obtain information on prior abuse and locations where it happened, details on injuries with statements from medical personnel, etc.

- Take steps to legally prevent the arrested abuser from being released on his or her own recognizance (O.R.) when appropriate.

- Seek bail enhancements where appropriate.

ASSIST PROSECUTION

Prepare for Court and Testimony

- Review all reports, photos and evidence.

- Make sure appropriate subpoenas have been served or due diligence efforts were made to serve witnesses.

- After arrest and up to point of prosecution, check on victim's safety periodically. Document/ investigate any threats, coercion or witness intimidation.

- Check with the Deputy D.A. before the court date and determine if he or she requires any assistance or has any suggestions.

- Enhance your courtroom testimony abilities by interviewing experienced officers and detectives and by reading training materials related to courtroom testimony. Attend other domestic violence courtroom hearings and trials as an unrelated observer to gain insight and knowledge of such proceedings.

- After the case is settled in court assist the Deputy D.A. in any steps necessary to obtain further court protective orders for victim(s). Educate any related victims or witnesses on what to do to protect themselves and how to report any threats, coercion or intimidation to law enforcement immediately.

USE LAWFUL MEANS TO PREVENT BAIL, OWN RECOGNIZANCE (O.R.) OR OTHER RELEASE OF THE DV ABUSER

CA Penal Code 853.6(a) – Citation (O.R.) Restrictions on Violation of a DV Protective Order & Misdemeanor DV Arrest

- In any case in which a person is arrested for a misdemeanor violation of a protective court order involving domestic violence (DV as defined in PC 13700 [b]) or arrested for domestic violence abuse (direct abuse or violation of a court protective order as defined in PC 13701), *the person shall be taken before a magistrate instead of being released on a citation (O.R.),* unless the arresting officer determines that there is not a reasonable likelihood that the offense will continue or resume or that the safety of persons or property would be imminently endangered by release of the person arrested.

PC 853.6 (a) indicates that agency policy and protocol shall be developed to assist officers in making such a determination as to whether there is or is not a reasonable likelihood that the offense will continue or resume or that the safety of persons or property would be imminently endangered by release of the person arrested.

See the California Commission on Peace Officer Standards and Training (POST) web site and view their "publications list", click on "list all" and locate "Guidelines for Law Enforcement Response to Domestic Violence". Also, try the direct link to the POST DV Guidelines -

http://www.post.ca.gov/Training/tps_bureau/domestic_violence/domestic-violence-manual_wv.pdf

Read POST guidelines to learn what considerations officers should use to determine when a citation (O.R.) release is not appropriate.

CA Penal Code 853.6(i) & 827.1 – Standard Reasons for Non-Release on Citation (O.R.) for Misdemeanor Arrest

- In addition to POST DV guideline restrictions on O.R. releases and the specific DV concerns listed in PC 853.6 (a), any misdemeanor citation (O.R.) release shall meet the requirements set forth in PC 853.6 (i) [reasons for non-release] and, if the misdemeanor charge was on an arrest warrant, PC 827.1 [conditions not eligible for O.R.].

CA Penal Code 1270.1 – Citation (O.R) Release Restriction on Violation of a DV Protective Order or DV Battery Arrest

- *Prohibits O.R. release of a person arrested for PC 243 (e)(1).* This Section also prevents O.R. release for a violation of PC 273.6 <u>until a hearing is held in open court if</u>, "the detained person made threats to kill or harm, has engaged in violence against, or has gone to the residence or workplace of, the protected party".

- *What Does this Mean?:* This is extremely important because if a person is arrested for PC 243 (e) (1) or PC 273.6 (if the PC 273.6 arrestee made threats to kill or harm, has engaged in violence against, or has gone to the residence or workplace of the protected party); <u>then the arrested person can not be released on O.R. until he or she has a hearing in open court</u> (thus they wait in jail until that hearing has occurred).

CA Penal Code 1270.1 – Bail Release Restriction When Bail is Modified Higher or Lower than the Standard Bail Schedule

- <u>Before any person</u> who is arrested for any of the following crimes <u>may be released on bail</u> in an amount that <u>is either more or less</u> than the amount contained in the schedule of bail for the offense, <u>a hearing shall be held in open court</u> before the magistrate or judge:

- A serious felony, as defined in Penal Code subdivision (c) of Section 1192.7, or a violent felony, as defined in subdivision (c) of Section 667.5, but not including a violation of subdivision (a) of Section 460 (residential burglary).

- A violation of Penal Code Section 136.1 where punishment is imposed pursuant to subdivision (c) of Section 136.1, 262, 273.5, 422 (where the offense is punished as a felony) or 646.9.

- A violation of paragraph (1) of Penal Code subdivision (e) of Section 243.

- A violation of Penal Code Section 273.6 if the detained person made threats to kill or harm, has engaged in violence against, or has gone to the residence or workplace of, the protected party.

- *What Does this Mean?*: This is extremely important if a person arrested has had his or her bail modified (usually a request by a law enforcement agency to have the bail "enhanced"). Because once such a modification takes place for an arrest on one or more of the listed charges/ conditions listed in PC 1270.1, then <u>the arrested person can not be released on bail until he or she has a hearing in open court</u> (thus they wait in jail until that hearing has occurred).

VIII. DOMESTIC VIOLENCE SCENARIOS – AND TENANCY ISSUES

SCENARIOS

Officers are sent to a house on a disturbance call. Upon arrival, they see Mary who is crying and bleeding from the nose and has a stab wound to the back. She says her husband, Fred, came home late and had been drinking; he punched her in the nose, got a knife and stabbed her between the shoulder blades as she tried to run out of the door.

- This would clearly be a DV crime of violence or injury.

- This is, of course, a PC 273.5 (a), PC 245 (a) (1) or PC 664/187 crime.

What type of DV crime (assault & injury similar to the case above) by abuser upon the victim be, if the victim was never a cohabitant or married with the abuser, never had a child with the abuser, but was pregnant by the abuser from dating?

- This is, of course, a DV crime.

    o *But it would not be PC 273.5 (a) until the child is born.*

    o *It would be crime of PC 245(a)(1) or PC 664/ 187.*

    o *Remember, all PC 273.5 (a) is DV, but not all DV is PC 273.5 (a).*

What if this DV involved Fred & Sam in intimate relations?

- Same sex qualifies as a domestic violence relationship.

What if victim Mary (assault & injury similar to the case above) was 70 years old? Would there be any other considerations regarding the case?

- The investigation should include PC 368 (b)(1), inflicting unjustifiable physical pain or mental suffering, on any elder or dependent adult under circumstances or conditions likely to produce great bodily harm or death.

In the course of the investigation (assault & injury similar to the case above), you learn that Suzie (their daughter) age 5, was in the kitchen and saw the attack. Would there be any other considerations regarding the case?

- The investigation should include P.C. 273a (a) or (b), child endangering. That crime includes inflicting mental suffering or placing child in a situation where his or her health is or may be endangered.

- Always include the names and ages of any minors who were present or witnessed the offense. This is very important as this may trigger P.C. 1170.76 (in some cases) which courts shall consider as a circumstance in aggravation for imposing the high term sentence.

  o *This information is also necessary to assist authorities in getting proper victim services to the children.*

  o *In some incidents, children present during DV crimes may affect how the District Attorney handles the case.*

As you leave with Fred, who is under arrest, (assault & injury similar to the case above), he turns and yells to Mary, "Bitch, wait till I get out! You better keep your mouth shut! You're dead!" Are there any additional charges or other considerations?

- P.C. 422 – (Criminal threats).

- P.C. 136.1(b)(1) or 140(a) – (Threats or intimidation of witness).

Should you charge one or multiple offenses when possible?

- Stack them all - let the D.A. decide

  o *Charges help clarify what type of case is being dealt with.*

  o *Charges get the attention of the D.A., Probation, & the Court.*

  o *Charges may influence the setting of bail.*

  o *Charges may assist in obtaining a protection order.*

  o *Complete charges reflect on the abuser's CII Rap Sheet and thus paint a clearer picture of the abuser for law enforcement and prosecutors in the future.*

After husband Fred was arrested, a protective order to protect Mary and Suzie was issued and served. Fred then bailed out. Over the next two days, Fred came to their house 3 times, phoned Mary at work on 4 different occasions & drove by Suzie's preschool where a teacher saw him. Fred told the teacher, "I'm going to kill Mary!"

In addition to a violation of a protective order, what other crimes may be present?

- PC 646.9(a) – Stalking.

- PC 646.9(b) – Stalking while there is a restraining or protective order (civil or criminal) in effect prohibiting the suspect from stalking.

- PC 653m (c)(1) – Annoying phone calls at work while there is a restraining or protective order (civil or criminal) in effect prohibiting communicating with protected party.

- PC 422 – Criminal threats.

TENANCY ISSUES AND KEEPING THE PEACE

Direct a person who is not lawfully present/ residing at the location to leave when: (1) a complaining party is lawfully present/ residing at the location, and (2) the complaining party has told that person to leave.

- Lawful possession may be ascertained by statements, rent receipts, lease, deed, utility receipts, verification by apartment manager, etc.

- Officers should stand by for a reasonable amount of time to keep the peace while the person not in lawful possession removes essential belongings.

- If the subject does not leave upon request by the complainant in lawful possession of the premises _and_ the officer, the person is subject to arrest under Penal Code Sections 602(o) and 602.5(a) or (b). Private person's arrests are encouraged in these cases, but are not required, if a misdemeanor is committed in the officer's presence.

- If the complainant requesting removal of the subject cannot show proof of lawful possession but insist that he or she is the person in lawful possession and insists upon making a private person's arrest, that person may do so. Officers shall follow the law as outlined in Penal Code Sections 142, 837 and 847.

- These are suggested procedures. All officers should follow their agencies procedures regarding such incidents as described herein. _FOLLOW YOUR AGENCY'S POLICY ON PRIVATE PERSONS ARRESTS._

IX. VICTIM ASSISTANCE

LAW AND PROFESSIONAL MANDATES (SEE POST GUIDELINES) REQUIRE PEACE OFFICERS TO PROVIDE VICTIMS OF DV WITH ASSISTANCE – SEE PC SECTIONS 13701 (c) AND 264.2 (a) FOR SPECIFIC DETAILS

Emergency assistance

- Peace officers must provide to DV victims:

  o *Medical care*

  o *Transportation to a hospital for treatment when necessary*

  o *Transportation to a shelter*

  o *Peace officer standby for removing personal property*

  o *Assistance in safe passage out of victim's residence (or other location)*

Informational assistance

- Peace officers must provide to DV victims:

  o *The report number and directions to the proper investigation unit*

  o *Written statements and notices*

    1. *Despite arrest, the abuser may be released at any time*

    2. *Information on how to contact victim services in the community*

    3. *Information on how to contact victim shelters in the community*

    4. *Information on the State of California victim compensation program and its phone number*

    5. *Information that the victim may ask the D.A. to file a criminal complaint*

    6. *Information that the victim has a right to go to superior court and file a petition requesting orders of relief, including but not limited to a restraining order – see PC Section 13701 (c)(9)(F) for details*

    7. *A statement informing the victim of the right to file a civil suit for losses suffered as a result of the abuse – see PC Section 13701 (c)(9)(G) for details*

    8. *In the case of an alleged violation of subdivision (e) of PC 243 or PC Sections 261, 261.5, 262, 273.5, 286, 288a, or 289, a "Victims of Domestic Violence" card which shall include specific victim*

assistance information – see PC Section 13701 (c)(9)(H) for details

- Providing the above victim information assistance is not just a good idea . . . *it is the law*. If a law enforcement agency or officers are not providing this information, they are violating State of California law and POST guidelines.

- A law enforcement agency could use a victim information page or form instead of a "card". See a sample – DV Victim Information form – near the end of this book.

- *Protect victim's identity in certain crimes* (some of the crimes are DV related and some are not – examples are PC Sections 261, 262, 273.5, 646.9) *when confidentiality laws permit*. Have victim complete the appropriate confidentiality form as required in PC Section 293 & Government Code Section 6254 (f). See a sample – Victim Confidentiality Request form – near the end of this book.

X. STRANGULATION INVESTIGATION

STRANGULATION VICTIMS MAY NOT HAVE VISIBLE INJURIES

Think back to how many times you, the officer, arrived at a DV incident where the victim (most often a female) has told you the abuser (most often a male) "choked" her. However, it is then noticed that there are no visible marks on the neck of the victim. Many times the officers (and I did the same thing early in my career) disbelieved the victim based upon that lack of visible marks.

The reality is this: _In 80 - 85% of strangulation cases, there are minor or no external signs visible immediately following the strangulation._ However, there may be internal injuries visible to a doctor using a laryngoscope. That's why it is so important to get the victim of strangulation to the emergency room so a doctor may conduct an examination. The doctor's statement & medical findings may include "internal bruising and injuries consistent with strangulation."

Visible signs consistent with strangulation (where present) may be: redness or swelling on the neck, hoarseness, swallowing problems, difficulty with breathing, involuntary urination or defecation, blood red eyes due to capillary rupture, and tiny red spots (petechiae) of ruptured capillaries found in and around the eyes, neck, face or area above the constriction point.

Strangulation is a serious charge that demands the investigation be handled professionally and with attention paid to details.

Key point – Strangulation is often overlooked & under-reported.

Key point – Audio or video record all statements if possible.

Check list for investigation and reporting:

- General Investigation – Suspect's Statements – Documentation

  o _Document all parties' spontaneous statements (for suspect - before and after arrest)._

  o _Note relationship of suspect to victim._

  o _Note prior DV calls for service per PC 13730._

  o _Describe suspect's: location at your first contact, demeanor, emotional and physical condition and any injuries._

  o _Note suspect's drug and alcohol use, if any._

  o _Probable cause for arrest may exist for <u>one or more</u> of the charges listed below when there is evidence of strangulation and the victim survives:_

1. *PC 273.5 (a) Corporal Injury on Spouse/ Cohabitant*

2. *PC 245 (a)(1) Assault with Deadly Weapon/ Force*

3. *PC 664-187 Attempted Murder*

o *Attempt Miranda interview after arrest.*

o *Protect victim's identity in certain crimes (PC 273.5 (a) applies) when confidentiality laws permit. Have victim complete the appropriate confidentiality form. See PC 293 & Government Code 6254 (f) (2) (3).*

o *Obtain an EPO when ever possible. Follow law re: telling a DV victim of the right to request an EPO.*

o <u>*When an arrest is made*</u>*, give the victim a V.I.N.E. information form/ sheet (or equivalent, if your county has such a V.I.N.E. system) as this allows the victim to be notified if the abuser is released from jail.*

o *Note additional contact numbers (friend, family member, victim's cell number) for the victim as he or she may not return to their home or work.*

- <u>Victim's Symptoms and Condition</u>

o *Is victim alert, oriented?*

o *Does victim have: difficulty breathing, coughing, a choking sensation, hoarseness, loss of voice, or is coughing up blood?*

o *Is victim faint, dizzy, light-headed, or had a loss of consciousness?*

o *Did victim vomit or have a loss of control of bowel or bladder?*

o *Is there neck pain, swelling, discomfort, or swallowing problems?*

o *Are there any visible injuries, redness, swelling, bruises, bites, cuts, scratches, red spots on face, neck or in eyes (petechiae)? [Note that it is NOT unusual for a victim of strangulation to have no external injuries on the neck].*

o *Are there visible "pattern to injuries", such as: finger grip marks or cord marks? If so, note size and location upon the victim's neck.*

o *Is there any evidence of drug or alcohol use by the victim prior to strangulation?*

o *Is there soreness of the throat, raspy voice, or swollen eyes or eyelids?*

o *Pre-existing neck injuries or illnesses.*

o *Taking any prescribed medications.*

- <u>Victim's Investigation - Statements – Documentation – Very Important</u>

o *Document all spontaneous statements.*

- How were you strangled? With one hand, two hands, forearm, rope, chain, cord? Ask the victim to describe how and what was used.

- Did the suspect say anything while he (or she) was strangling you?

- Victims may use the word "choke" instead of the word "strangle". *When quoting the victim* (in reports and in court), use whatever the word the victim used to describe the act.

- However, *officers* (for police reports & courtroom testimony) *should use the word "strangulation" not "choking"* when describing what type of act they are investigating.

  1. Information for officers: *The criminal act is one of "strangulation", not "choking".* A person knowingly strangles another person. "Choking" is usually accidental as when a person chokes on food, other object or by some mishap or medical condition.

- Did the suspect shake you while he (or she) was strangling you?

- Were you thrown against the wall or floor? Describe how and what happened.

- How many times were you strangled? Describe each event and method.

- How much pressure was used? Was the pressure continuous?

- What were you thinking while you were being strangled?

- What made the suspect stop?

  1. Ask victim what (if anything) he or she did to stop the assault and what was the result.

- Are you having any difficulty breathing now?

- Did you have any difficulty breathing during the assault?

- How did you feel during the assault? Did you feel faint, dizzy, nauseous *or lose consciousness?*

- Ask about prior incidents of strangulation or "choking".

- Evidence

  - Photograph victim and suspect (& marks) and areas of complaints of pain. Photograph any objects used for the strangulation.

    1. Re-do victim follow-up photographs 48 hours later to retake photos in areas of the complaint of pain & injury.

  - Seize and book evidence, weapons and any items used in the assault.

  - Document marks, injuries, etc. on a body diagram.

1. *Was the suspect wearing any rings? Check for marks from these items.*

2. *Check behind the victim's ears, and neck, chin, jaw, eyelids, chest, and shoulders for marks, petechiae, etc.*

o *Arrange for medical treatment; ask for a laryngoscope exam in a hospital ER (laryngoscope exam is a fiber optic exam of the throat to show interior injury not visible from exterior).*

o *Have victim sign a medical records release when possible, even if the victim does not obtain treatment right away (victim may obtain treatment at a later time).*

o *Find, list and interview any witnesses.*

1. *Find, list and interview the reporting party (RP).*

2. *Find, list and interview any children who were witnesses or just even present at the location.*

3. *List relatives who arrived on scene after the crime and who are not witnesses.*

o *List any and all agencies on scene: other police agencies, fire department, private ambulances and children services.*

o *Identify treating doctors.*

XI. DOMESTIC VIOLENCE POLICY & REPORTING REQUIREMENTS

MINIMAL POLICY AND REPORTING REQUIREMENTS (PC 13700 – PC 13701 – PC 13702 – PC 13730)

Remember that the following are "minimal" policy & reporting requirements mandated by state law. Police agencies could require additional information to be included in their particular reporting procedures.

Basic definition of "domestic violence" under California Law

- *"Domestic Violence"* (for criminal purposes)– means _abuse_ committed against an adult or a minor who is a spouse, former spouse, cohabitant, former cohabitant, or person with whom the suspect has had a child, or is having or has had a dating or engagement relationship. For purposes of this document, *"cohabitant"* means two unrelated adult persons living together for a substantial period of time resulting in some permanency of relationship.

  The above definition also applies to domestic violence between persons of the same gender and to any minor, emancipated or not.

  "Abuse" – means intentionally or recklessly _causing or attempting to cause_ bodily injury, or placing another person in reasonable apprehension of imminent serious bodily injury to himself, herself, or another.

- *Remember*: Domestic violence relationships defined for criminal purposes, *as listed above*, are in PC Section 13700. _However, the definition of domestic violence relationships for obtaining an EPO is greatly broadened._ They include the relationships as defined in PC Section 13700 _and_ those defined in FC Section 6211 (also see related FC 6203, 6205, 6209, 6210). **See "Obtaining an Emergency Protective Order (EPO)" section listed earlier.**

Basic policy requirements mandated by California law

- Every law enforcement agency <u>shall</u> develop, adopt and implement written policies and standards for officers' response to DV calls.

- Policies <u>shall</u> reflect that domestic violence is alleged criminal conduct.

- Policies <u>shall</u> reflect that a request for assistance in a situation involving domestic violence is the same as any other request for assistance where violence has occurred.

- Policies <u>shall encourage the arrest</u> of domestic violence offenders if there is probable cause that an offense has been committed.

- Policies <u>shall require the arrest</u> of an offender, absent exigent circumstances, if there is probable cause that a protective order (per PC 13701) or restraining order (per PC 836 [c] [1]) has been knowingly violated.

- The combination of authorities listed in PC 836 (c) (1) and PC 13701 make the mandated arrest requirement apply to court orders issued by a court of this state, court of another state, a commonwealth, territory, or insular possession subject to the jurisdiction of the United States, a military tribunal, or a tribe.

- <u>Policies shall discourage, when appropriate, but not prohibit, dual arrests.</u> Peace officers shall make reasonable efforts to identify the dominant (AKA primary) aggressor in any incident. The dominant aggressor is the person determined to be the most significant, rather than the first, aggressor. In identifying the dominant aggressor, an officer shall consider the intent of the law to protect victims of domestic violence from continuing abuse, the threats creating fear of physical injury, the history of domestic violence between the persons involved, an whether either person acted in self-defense.

  - The combination of authorities listed in PC 836 (c) (3) and PC 13701 indicate the same considerations shall apply in situations where mutual protective orders have been issued.

- <u>Every law enforcement agency in the state shall develop, adopt, and implement written policies and standards for dispatchers' response to domestic violence calls.</u> These policies shall reflect that calls reporting threatened, imminent, or ongoing domestic violence, and the violation of any protection or restraining orders issued by the courts shall be ranked among the highest priority calls. Dispatchers are not required to verify the validity of the court order before responding to the request for assistance (PC 13702).

- <u>Policies shall be in writing</u> and be available to the public upon request <u>and shall include specific standards</u> for the following [summarized – see PC 13701 (c) for details].

  - Felony, misdemeanor and citizen arrests.

  - Verification and enforcement of court issued protective and restraining orders.

  - Cite and release policies.

  - Emergency assistance to victims.

  - Assisting victims with pursuing criminal options, such as providing report numbers and directing victim to the proper investigating unit.

  - Furnishing written notice to victims at the scene, including but not limited to: informing the victim the suspect may be released at any time; emergency, shelter, and California state victim's compensation program contact phone numbers; notice that victim may contact the district attorney to file a criminal complaint; a statement informing the victim of the right to go to the superior court and request a court order for relief in a variety of areas (see code); a statement informing the victim of the right to file a civil suit for losses suffered; the name and phone numbers of local county hotlines for shelters and counseling centers along with their 24-hour telephone numbers; a statement on the proper procedures for a victim to follow after a sexual assault; and simple definitions that sexual assault by a person who is known to the victim or who is the spouse of the victim, is a crime.

  - Writing of reports.

Police reporting shall include at minimum the following

- All domestic violence-related calls for assistance <u>shall</u> be supported with a written incident report.

- Monthly, the total number of domestic violence calls received and the numbers of those cases involving weapons <u>shall</u> be compiled by each law enforcement agency and submitted to the State Attorney General.

- The Attorney General <u>shall</u> report annually to the Governor, the Legislature, and the public the total number of domestic violence-related calls received by California law enforcement agencies: the number of cases involving weapons, and a breakdown of calls received by agency, city, and county.

  - *This means that local police agencies <u>must report</u> the above required subject matter so the Attorney General can make the required annual report to the state.*

- <u>In all incidents of domestic violence, a report shall be written and shall be identified on the face of the report as a domestic violence incident.</u> The report <u>shall</u> include <u>at least</u> all of the following:

  - *A notation of whether the officer or officers who responded to the domestic violence call observed any signs that the alleged abuser was under the influence of alcohol or a controlled substance.*

  - *A notation of whether the officer or officers who responded to the domestic violence call determined if any law enforcement agency had previously responded to a domestic violence call at the same address involving the same alleged abuser or victim.*

  - *A notation of whether the officer or officers who responded to the domestic violence call found it necessary, for the protection of the peace officer or other persons present, to inquire of the victim, the alleged abuser, or both, whether a firearm or other deadly weapon was present at the location, and, if there is an inquiry, whether that inquiry disclosed the presence of a firearm or other deadly weapon. Any firearm or other deadly weapon discovered by an officer at the scene of a DV incident shall be subject to confiscation pursuant to PC Section 12028.5.*

Note: The above required information meets a minimal mandate – Agency's should include additional information in reports

- <u>The reporting requirements listed on DV report forms used in many law enforcement agencies in California contain the following, in addition to the above.</u> This information should be gathered consistently so that a proper picture can be drawn of the exact circumstances involved in the domestic violence incident. Officers can not possibly remember all of the questions necessary. <u>Most law enforcement agencies use a check-off-the-box type form.</u>

  - *A notation of whether the officer or officers who responded to the domestic violence call observed any signs that the alleged abuser <u>or victim</u> was under the influence of alcohol or a controlled substance.*

  - *A notation indicating the domestic violence relationship, i.e.; spouse – former spouse – parent of a child from relationship - cohabitants - former cohabitant – dating – former dating – same sex partnership – minor – other person, child or relationship as described in FC 6205 through 6211 or PC 836(d). The relationships listed, allow the DV report to cover crimes and the documentation of DV incidents to obtain a court restraining or protective order that may or may not be a crime [FC 6203 (c) – "to place a person in reasonable apprehension of imminent serious bodily injury to that person or to another"]. Remember, the Family Code allows expanded definitions of DV relationships to provide the issuance of court protective orders. <u>All such incidents should be documented as "domestic violence-related" incidents.</u>*

- A notation indicating that a victim information card or form was issued covering topics such as: victim rights, victim services and resources, VINE form, etc., as mentioned earlier.

- A notation indicating that a _victim confidentiality form was issued as required_ by PC 293 & Government Code 6254 (f) (2) (3).

- A notation indicating victim's condition; i.e., calm, nervous, complaint of pain, visible injury, etc.

- A notation indicating suspect's condition; i.e., calm, nervous, complaint of pain, visible injury, etc.

- A notation indicating what type of medical services were rendered to the victim or suspect, if any.

- A notation of other information required as may be determined by the individual agency.

Sample domestic violence report/ forms

- See sample – _DV Crime/ Incident report – near end of book._

- See sample - _Verbal Service of a Restraining Order by a Peace Officer form – near end book._

- See sample – _Victim Confidentiality Request form – near end of book._

- See sample – _DV Victim Information form – near end of book._

XII. DOMESTIC VIOLENCE & THE LAW ENFORCEMENT SUSPECT - POLICY

SUGGESTED MINIMAL POLICY FOR THE DV LAW ENFORCMENT SUSPECT

The following is a suggested policy only. Peace officers should always follow their respective agencies' policies and procedures.

- All domestic violence incidents involving law enforcement personnel shall be handled according to standard policy.

- There shall be no deviation from standard policy merely because the suspect is employed by a law enforcement agency.

- Special notifications and review

    1. *Any officer investigating an alleged incident of DV involving a law enforcement employee suspect shall contact his / her (reporting agency's) on-duty supervisor as soon as possible.*

    2. *The investigating agency should notify the suspect's employing agency as soon as possible after the incident or initial report.*

    3. *All incidents involving suspects who are sworn peace officers or reserve peace officers will be reviewed by the District Attorney's Office.*

This *DV law enforcement suspect policy* (in substance) has been provided by permission and courtesy of the Police Chiefs' Association of Santa Clara County's "Domestic Violence Protocol for Law Enforcement" – 2007 – by permission of Chair, Chief Bruce Cumming, Morgan Hill Police Department (per Commander David Swing, Morgan Hill P.D.)

XIII. DOMESTIC VIOLENCE & THE MILITARY SUSPECT - POLICY

SUGGESTED MINIMAL POLICY FOR THE DV U.S. MLITARY & ACTIVATED OR ON-DUTY NATIONAL GUARD SUSPECT

The following is a suggested policy only. Peace officers should always follow their respective agencies' policies and procedures.

- All domestic violence incidents involving United States Military and activated or on-duty State National Guard personnel shall be handled according to standard policy if:

  1. *The incident occurred outside the boundaries of a military facility; and*

  2. *Local law enforcement is acting within its jurisdictional boundaries and not in an area controlled by the military during war or marshal law.*

- The intent of this policy is to eliminate all informal referrals, diversions or report taking omissions in the handling of domestic violence incidents involving military personnel.

- No informal agreements with military police or a suspect's commanding officer shall take precedence over a suspect's arrest and prosecution by non-military authorities.

This *DV military suspect policy* (in substance) has been provided by permission and courtesy of the Police Chiefs' Association of Santa Clara County's "Domestic Violence Protocol for Law Enforcement" – 2007 – by permission of Chair, Chief Bruce Cumming, Morgan Hill Police Department (per Commander David Swing, Morgan Hill P.D.)

XIV. STATEMENTS – IMPORTANCE OF OBTAINING STATEMENTS

VICTIM STATEMENTS

Key point – Audio or video record all statements when possible.

- Document *spontaneous statements* made upon first contact. Spontaneous statements are an exception to the hearsay rule per Evidence Code 1240. A judge *may* decide to allow the officer to testify to hearsay statements even if the person making the original statement does not testify.

- Consider questions for victim similar to those outlined in Chapter X – Strangulation.

- Book as evidence taped investigation statements and taped phone calls made to the station by the victim.

WITNESS AND REPORTING PARTY STATEMENTS

Key point – Audio or video record all statements when possible.

- Document *spontaneous statements* made upon first contact. Spontaneous statements are an exception to the hearsay rule per Evidence Code 1240. A judge *may* decide to allow the officer to testify to hearsay statements even if the person making the original statement does not testify.

- Consider questions for witnesses and reporting parties such as: how did they first become aware of the incident; what do they know of the history of the involved parties; what exactly did they see happen today; what did they hear the suspect and victim say; and (if there are children involved) do they know how the children are treated? Some of the questions listed for "victims" outlined in Chapter X – Strangulation, may be similar to questions to use for witnesses and reporting parties.

- Book as evidence taped investigation statements and taped phone calls made to the station by witnesses and reporting parties.

CHILDREN AS WITNESSES – STATEMENTS

Key point – Audio or video record all statements when possible.

- Document *spontaneous statements* made upon first contact. Spontaneous statements are an exception to the hearsay rule per Evidence Code 1240. A judge *may* decide to allow the officer to testify to hearsay statements even if the person making the original statement does not testify.

- Interview away from the parents.

- Speak to child's level and sit or kneel down.

- Comfort and calm the child.

  o *Assure the child that he/ she did nothing wrong.*

  o *Assure the child that he/ she is not in trouble with their parents or the police.*

- o *Assure the child that this (incident) is not their fault.*

- o *Assure the child that you want to help.*

- o *Determine (carefully) if they have been the victim of abuse.*

- Describe the child's demeanor.

- Quote _specifically_ the child's statements (no cop talk).

- Determine if they have talked to anyone outside the home about these problems. _And if so . . . who?_

- Ask them if they are afraid . . . _if so, of who?_

- All identifying information on the children must be in police report (whether or not you interview them).

- The children can tell you what you need to know.

  - o *They are good witnesses!*

  - o *Think about spontaneous statements from the 911 call tape if the child spoke on the phone to police personnel.*

  - o *If you start to give up on these DV calls, remember the children.*

  - o *If you think it's a waste of time to bother interviewing children, think again. Often they are surprisingly articulate.*

SUSPECT STATEMENTS

Key point – Audio or video record all statements when possible.

- Document _spontaneous statements_ made upon first contact (and even later after arrest). Spontaneous statements are an exception to the hearsay rule per Evidence Code 1240. A judge _may_ decide to allow the officer to testify to hearsay statements even if the person making the original statement does not testify.

- Book as evidence taped investigation statements and taped phone calls made to the station by the suspect.

Often, there are up to four (4) ways to get incriminating statements from a suspect.

- **When first arriving (#1) – listen and note the initial spontaneous (and contemporaneous) statements made by both parties.** When a suspect is identified, these statements may be used against him or her later at trial as they are not the result of any interrogation or prompting.

- **Whenever possible (#2) – interview the suspect prior to arrest.** This is for obtaining pre-arrest investigatory statements which are admissible in court.

- **Shortly after arrest, (#3) – listen to what the suspect says spontaneously.** Often, the abuser will tell you he or she "did it". Just listen, don't question. These types of post arrest spontaneous statements are very valuable to use in prosecutions. Quote suspect verbatim. _You must not elicit statements_.

- **After arrest, (#4) – attempt Miranda waiver and interview.**

SPONTANEOUS STATEMENTS – RELATING TO WITNESSES – ADDITIONAL INFO

Spontaneous Statements – 1240 of the Evidence Code.

- _Spontaneous statements_ are an exception to the hearsay rule per Evidence Code 1240. A judge _may_ decide to allow the officer to testify to hearsay statements even if the person making the original statement does not testify.

- Spontaneous statements purport to narrate, describe, or explain an event, act or condition perceived by the victim or witness and made spontaneously while that person was under the stress of excitement caused by that perception.

  - _Relates to a startling event which produces nervous excitement and makes the statements spontaneous and made without reflection._

  - _The utterance was made before there was time to contrive or misrepresent._

  - _The utterance relates to the startling event. It is irrelevant whether the victim or witness is available at trial to testify_

  - _The crucial element in determining whether a declaration is sufficiently reliable to be admissible under the spontaneous statement exception to the hearsay rule, is not the nature of the statement, but the mental state of the speaker._

  - _Cover in your report: Who said it? – When did they say it? – What was going on at the time? – What were they doing when they said it? – What exactly did they say (be very accurate, quote, tape, etc.)?_

  - _A child may make admissible spontaneous statements, if those statements would otherwise be admissible by others._

- Spontaneous statements can be extremely valuable in prosecuting a criminal case and yet they are often overlooked and misunderstood by reporting officers.

XV. DOMESTIC VIOLENCE RELATIONSHIP/ COMMON CHARGE CHART – QUICK REFERENCE

No Injury Charge	Relationship	Injury Charge
PC 243(e)(1)	**Married** **Past or Present**	PC 273.5
PC 243(e)(1)	***Cohabitant** **Past or Present** (* as defined in P.C.13700)	PC 273.5
PC 243(e)(1)	**Child in Common**	PC 273.5
PC 243(e)(1)	**Engaged** **Past or Present**	PC 243(e)(1) & w/ serious injury PC 243 (d)
PC 243(e)(1)	**Dating** **Past or Present**	PC 243(e)(1) & w/ serious injury PC 243 (d)

Circumstances may allow for other or additional charges.

XVI. MISDEMEANOR ARREST AUTHORITY PC 836 (d) – DOMESTIC VIOLENCE EXPANDED RELATIONSHIP GUIDE – QUICK REFERENCE

PC 836 (d): Authority for <u>misdemeanor</u> arrest, <u>not committed</u> in a peace officer's presence, when a suspect commits an <u>assault</u> or <u>battery</u> upon the following:

- Current or former spouse
- Fiancé or Fiancée
- Current or former cohabitant defined in Section 6209 Family Code
- Person whom suspect is having or had an engagement relationship
- Person whom suspect is having or had a dating relationship, as defined in Section 243 (f) PC
- Person with whom suspect had a child
- A child of the suspect
- A child of a person in one of the above categories
- Any other person related to the suspect by consanguinity or affinity within the second degree
- Any person 65 years of age or older and who is related to the suspect by blood or legal guardianship

<u>AND</u>

When both of the following circumstances apply:

1) Officer has probable cause to believe the suspect has committed the assault or battery, whether or not it has in fact been committed.

2) Officer makes the arrest as soon as probable cause arises to believe the person committed the assault or battery

XVII. DOMESTIC VIOLENCE RELATED CHARGES / QUICK REFERENCE

ALWAYS CHECK THE LAW (CODE SECTION) FOR SPECIFIC ELEMENTS (COMMON CHARGES - NOT ALL POSSIBLE CHARGES ARE LISTED)

- PC 136.1 (b)(1) - THREAT OR INTIMIDATION OF A WITNESS
- PC 136.5 - POSSESSION OF A DEADLY WEAPON W/ INTENT TO DISSUADE WITNESS
- PC 140(a) - USE OR THREAT OF USE OF FORCE AGAINST A WITNESS OR VICTIM
- PC 166 (a)(4) - MISDEMEANOR VIOLATION OF A COURT ORDER
- PC 166 (c)(4) - FEL. VIOLATION OF CRIMINAL PROTECTIVE/ RESTR'G ORDER
- PC 187 - MURDER
- PC 203 - MAYHEM - DEPRIVES ANOTHER OF MEMBER OF BODY, EYE, CUTS TONGUE
- PC 207 - KIDNAPPING
- PC 236/ 237 - FALSE IMPRISONMENT
- PC 243 (e) - DOMESTIC VIOLENCE BATTERY
- PC 243(d) - BATTERY W/ SERIOUS INJURY
- PC 245 - ADW (VARIOUS WAYS/ METHODS)
- PC 246 - SHOOTING AT AN INHABITED DWELLING
- PC 246.3 - DISCHARGE FIREARM WITH GROSS NEGLIGENCE
- PC 246.3 (b) - DISCHARGE BB DEVICE W/ GROSS NEGLIGENCE WHICH MAY INJURE
- PC 261-262 - VARIOUS RAPE CRIMES
- PC 273.5 (a) - CORPORAL INJURY ON SPOUSE/COHABITANT/CHILD IN COMMON
- PC 273a (a) & (b) - CHILD ENDANGERING / ABUSE - MISDEMEANOR & FELONY
- PC 273.6 (a) - MISDEMEANOR VIOLATION OF A PROTECTIVE/ RESTRAINING ORDER
- PC 273.6 (d) - FEL. VIOL. OF A PROTECTIVE/ RESTRAINING ORDER - SEE CODE
- PC 273.6 (e) - FEL. VIOL. OF A PROTECTIVE/ RESTRAINING ORDER - SEE CODE
- PC 368 - ELDER ABUSE - MISDEMEANOR & FELONY
- PC 417 - BRANDISHING A WEAPON - SEE CODE
- PC 418 - FORCIBLE ENTRY INTO LANDS, HOME OF ANOTHER
- PC 422 - CRIMINAL THREATS (RENAMED FROM "TERRORIST THREATS")
- PC 459 - BURGLARY (SUSP. ENTERING STRUCTURE W/ INTENT TO COMMIT A FEL.)
- PC 591 - REMOVE, DAMAGE, OBSTRUCT PHONE, CABLE, ELECTRIC LINE
- PC 591.5 - REMOVE/ DESTROY WIRELESS COMM. DEVICE TO STOP USE TO CALL PD
- PC 594 - VANDALISM
- PC 596 - POISONING ANOTHERS ANIMAL
- PC 597 - CRUELTY TO ANIMALS
- PC 602 - TRESSPASS CRIMES - REVIEW LAW CAREFULLY FOR SPECIFIC CHARGE
- PC 602.5 - TRESSPASS & AGGRAVATED TRESSPASS INTO RESIDENCE
- PC 646.9 (a) - STALKING
- PC 646.9 (b) - STALKING W/ RESTR'G ORDER PROHIBITING SAME IS IN PLACE
- PC 653m - ANNOYING, REPEATED PHONE CALLS - (c)(1) AGAINST COURT ORDER
- PC 664 - ATTEMPT AT A CRIME, I.E. 664/ 187 - ATTEMPTED MURDER
- PC 12020 (a) POSSESSION OF ILLEGAL WEAPONS - SEE CODE
- PC 12021 (g) - POSSESS, PURCHASE OR RECEIVE FIREARM AGAINST COURT ORDER
- PC 12024 - POSSESSION OF A DEADLY WEAPON W/ INTENT TO USE IT
- PC 12025 - POSSESSION OF A CONCEALED FIREARM - SEE CODE
- PC 12031 - POSSESSION OF A LOADED FIREARM - SEE CODE

XVIII. SAMPLE OF DOMESTIC VIOLENCE FORMS

The following are **sample** DV related forms that may be useful to law enforcement in California. Many law enforcement agencies have and use forms similar to these below. If that is the case in your agency, please disregard these samples. However, it is this author's experience that some agencies do not have or do not have an updated:

- Specific **DV basic crime/ incident report form** covering specific required information as outlined in PC Section 13730.

- **DV victim information form (or card/ handout)** to provide specific required information to victims of DV as required in PC Sections 13701 and 264.2 (a).

- **DV crime victim (or other specified crime victim) confidentiality form** as required in PC Section 293 and Government Code Section 6254 (f).

- **Peace officer's verbal service of a restraining or protective order upon a restrained party form** as authorized or suggested in PC Section 836 (c)(2); Government Code Sections 6224, 6381, 6383 and 6385 and as suggested in POST DV Guidelines.

The *DV basic crime/ incident report form* is two-sided. This is mainly the "face page" or "synopsis" of the case and does not replace narrative or investigation pages. Each side is to be completed by the responsible peace officer prior to forwarding to his or her supervisor.

The *DV victim information form (statement)* is two-sided and the responsible peace officer would simply put his name, date and report number on the form prior to giving it to the victim. Please note there are boxes on the *basic DV crime report* where the officer should check off that this informational form was provided to the victim.

The *DV victim request for confidentially form* **and** the *peace officer's verbal service of a restraining or protective order form* are each two-sided. Side one of each form is to be completed by the responsible peace officer and side two of each form are the processing instructions for law enforcement personnel.

Note: These are just sample forms. Any form should be designed with the particular agency's needs in mind. Forms from other law enforcement agencies should also be considered.

DOMESTIC VIOLENCE BASIC
CRIME/ INCIDENT REPORT
FORM

(SIDE ONE & SIDE TWO ARE ON
THE NEXT TWO PAGES)

| Original | Supplemental | | ANYTOWN POLICE DEPARTMENT CA0000000
DOMESTIC VIOLENCE INCIDENT INVESTIGATION REPORT
(Use for DV crime, DV related crime, violation of an EPO or other DV related restraining order or to
document issuance of a DV EPO due to crime or threat) | | DR # | |

Code Section(s)	Crime			Classification	Area	RD
					VICTIM-FORM-ISSUED ☐ Yes ☐ No	

| Date and time occurred | Date and time reported | | VICT CONFIDENTIALITY FORM ISSUED
☐ Yes   ☐ No | V.I.N.E.-FORM-ISSUED
☐ Yes   ☐ No |

| Address # | Name of Street | | Type | City | Premise |

| S
T
A
T
U
S | APP-Applicant
ARA-Arrested Adult
ARJ-Arrested Juvenile
BIC-Bicyclist
COM-Complainant | DRI-Driver
EMP-Employee
MPR-Missing Person
OFA-Offender Adult
OFJ-Offender Juvenile | OTH-Other
OWN-Owner
LO-Legal Owner
PAR-Parent
PAS-Passenger | PED-Pedestrian
RES Respondent
PET-Petitioner
PO-Property Owner
POL-Police officer | PRP-Person Reporting
UNK-Unknown
RO-Registered Owner
RUN-Runaway
SUS-Suspect | VAD-Victim Adult
VBS-Victim Business
VJV-Victim Juvenile
WAN-Wanted
WAR-Warrant
WIT-Witness |

| Last Name | | First | | Middle | Status | Home Telephone
( ) |

| Address | City | State | Zip Code | Message/Pager /Other Phone
( ) |

| DOB | Age | Sex | Race | Height | Weight | Hair | Eyes | Facial Hair | Complexion | Build |

| Employer/School | Position | Address | City | State | Business Phone
( ) |

Describe Premises and Area Where Offense Occurred

Describe Briefly How Offense Was Committed

VICTIM/SUSPECT RELATIONSHIP (mark all that apply) ☐ Spouse   ☐ Former Spouse   ☐ Parents of Child from Relationship
☐ Cohabitants   ☐ Former Cohabitant   ☐ Dating – Engagement   ☐ Former Dating - Engagement Relationship   ☐ Same Sex
☐ Minor   [☐-Other Person, Child or Relationship as described in 6205 thru 6211 FC or 836(d) PC]

WEAPON USED BY SUSPECT IN CRIME OR ACT CAUSING ISSUANCE OF COURT ORDER OR HOW COURT ORDER WAS VIOLATED
(mark all that apply)   ☐ Firearm   ☐ Knife/Cutting Instrument   ☐ Other Deadly Weapon   ☐ Personal (hands/feet/etc)
☐ Verbal or Other Threats   Weapon Seized ☐ Yes ☐ No   ☐ Unknown Type Weapon   ☐ Act in Violation of Court Order

WEAPON(S) INQUIRY (mark "1" for all DV related calls – mark "2" **only** if answer to "1" is [X] Yes)
"1" Did officer(s) make inquiry of victim or abuser, or both, whether a firearm or other deadly weapon was present?   ☐ Yes   ☐ No
"2" If "1" is marked [X] Yes - did that inquiry disclose the presence of a firearm or other deadly weapon? ☐ Yes   ☐ No

RESTRAINING/PROTECTIVE ORDERS
Issued *Prior* to this Investigation   ☐ Yes ☐ No   ☐ Current   ☐ See Attached Copy   Served ☐ Yes ☐ No
Issued *During* this Investigation   ☐ Yes ☐ No   ☐ See Attached Copy   Served ☐ Yes ☐ No

| Last Name | | First | | Middle | Status | AKA's |

| Address | | | | | Home Telephone
( ) |

| DOB | Age | Race | Sex | Height | Weight | Hair | Eyes | Facial Hair | Complexion | Build |

| Citation # | Criminal ID# | Employer/School | | Position | Social Security # |

| Address | City | State | Zip Code | Business Telephone
( ) |

| VEH | Year | Make | Model | Style | License # | State | Vin# | Top Color | Bottom Color |

Further Action ☐ Yes   ☐ No   Other Agency _____   ☐ Check If Additional Subjects Involved

| Copies routed by | Typed By |

| Reporting Officer | ID# | Reviewed By | Date and Time |

-Side 1-

(2008)

WITNESSES/CHILDREN PRESENT – ANY CHILD ABUSE/ NEGLECT (mark all that apply)

Witnesses present during domestic violence: ☐ Yes ☐ No   Statements Taken: ☐ Yes ☐ No

Minor Children present (aggravation factor 1170.76 P.C.): ☐ Yes ☐ No   Statements Taken: ☐ Yes ☐ No

(Include the names and ages of any minor children in the report) Was a Child Abuse/ Neglect DR Taken ☐ Yes ☐ No - Report to CPS: ☐ Yes ☐ No

PREVIOUS POLICE REPORTS

Has Anytown Police previously responded to a domestic violence call at the <u>same address</u> involving the <u>same alleged abuser and/or victim:</u> ☐ Yes ☐ No

☐ Unknown (Explain in narrative)

MEDICAL TREATMENT (mark all that apply)

Paramedics on scene: ☐ Yes ☐ No   *IF YES :* ☐ FIRE DEPT ☐ OTHER:_____

VICTIM: ☐ None ☐ Paramedics ☐ Will seek own treatment ☐ Refused medical aid ☐ Hospital _____

SUSPECT: ☐ Not located ☐ None ☐ Paramedics ☐ Will seek own treatment ☐ Refused medical aid ☐ Hospital _____

VICTIM'S CONDITION (mark all that apply)

☐ Alcohol/Drugs

☐ Calm ☐ Apologetic ☐ Fearful ☐ Crying ☐ Angry ☐ Nervous ☐ Irrational ☐ Threatening

☐ Complaint of pain ☐ Bruise ☐ Abrasion ☐ Laceration ☐ Contusion

SUSPECT'S CONDITION (mark all that apply)

☐ Unknown / Not located   ☐ Not located but may have received injuries to:_____   ☐ Alcohol/Drugs

☐ Calm ☐ Apologetic ☐ Fearful ☐ Crying ☐ Angry ☐ Nervous ☐ Irrational ☐ Threatening

☐ Complaint of pain ☐ Bruise ☐ Abrasion ☐ Laceration ☐ Contusion

PHOTOGRAPHS / VIDEO

Photos of *VICTIM'S* injuries (or <u>lack</u> of injuries): ☐ Yes ☐ No   Type of images: ☐ 35mm ☐ Polaroid ☐ Digital ☐ Video

Photos of *SUSPECT'S* injuries (or <u>lack</u> of injuries): ☐ Yes ☐ No   Type of images: ☐ 35mm ☐ Polaroid ☐ Digital ☐ Video

No photos taken (explain):_____

"EVIDENCE COLLECTED" FOR DOMESTIC VIOLENCE RELATED SEX CRIMES ONLY (in below boxed area)

EVIDENCE COLLECTED

SEXUAL ASSAULT KIT: From *VICTIM* ☐ Yes ☐ No   From *SUSPECT* ☐ Yes ☐ No

Clothing (list items taken):_____

Bedding (list items taken):_____

Other (list items taken):_____

Did *VICTIM* shower: ☐ Yes ☐ No   Did *VICTIM* douche: ☐ Yes ☐ No   Notes:_____

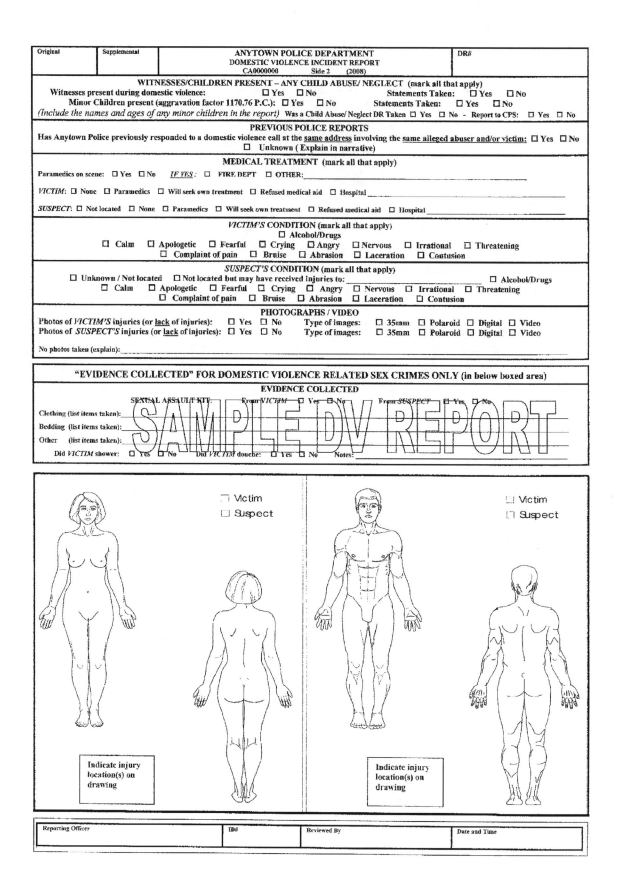

☐ Victim ☐ Suspect   ☐ Victim ☐ Suspect

Indicate injury location(s) on drawing   Indicate injury location(s) on drawing

Reporting Officer	ID#	Reviewed By	Date and Time

DOMESTIC VIOLENCE
VICTIM INFORMATION
FORM

(SIDE ONE & SIDE TWO ARE
ON THE NEXT TWO PAGES)

DOMESTIC VIOLENCE VICTIMS' INFORMATION HANDOUT

CONTACT OFFICER:_____ DATE:_____ REPORT # _____

PLEASE NOTE THE FOLLOWING DOMESTIC VIOLENCE VICTIM INFORMATION

What is "Domestic Violence"? Crimes of domestic violence is generally defined as abuse committed against an adult or minor who is a spouse, former spouse, cohabitant or former cohabitant (as defined in the Penal Code), or a person with whom the abuser has had a child or has had a dating relationship. In addition to the "crimes" of domestic violence in the Penal Code, the Family Code recognizes abuse committed against those mentioned above and others (such as persons related by blood or affinity within the second degree) as domestic violence for the purposes of judicial officers issuing restraining or protective orders against the abuser (suspect).

What is "Abuse"? It means intentionally or recklessly causing or attempting to cause bodily injury or placing another person in reasonable apprehension of imminent serious bodily injury to one's self or another.

Domestic violence or assault by a person who is known to the victim, including domestic violence or assault by a person who is the spouse of the victim, is a crime.

POLICE RESPONSE TO DOMESTIC VIOLENCE

It is the policy of the Anytown Police Department to respond to all calls involving domestic violence. If you believe you are a victim of domestic violence or reasonably fear that you are in imminent danger of serious injury, call the police department by dialing - 911 – **immediately**. The Anytown Police Department is committed to assisting you. Domestic violence is a complex and serious issue that you need to resolve. The information listed on both sides of this form outlines rights and responsibilities to protect you and your family from future victimization. Police will make a report of any domestic violence incidents they respond to even if you do not wish prosecution or arrest.

ARREST

There are two ways for the victim to have the attacker arrested. These are the police arrest and the private person's arrest (citizen arrest). The police may only arrest for a warrant issued for the attacker, a misdemeanor committed in their presence or if they have reasonable cause to believe that a felony has been committed. There are a few exceptions that allow police to arrest for certain misdemeanors not committed in their presence.

Every person may arrest another person who has committed a crime in his or her presence. Any time a victim is hit, beaten or assaulted, the attacker (suspect) is committing a crime in the victim's presence. The victim has a legal right to make a private person's arrest. The private person may only make a legal arrest for an actual crime, otherwise, the private person may be liable for false arrest or imprisonment.

If the alleged attacker (suspect) is arrested or officially restrained, it is important for the victim to know that restrained person may be released at anytime. If you are injured, notify the police immediately and they will assist you in obtaining appropriate medical attention. For information about the California victim's compensation program, you may contact 1-(911) 911-1111 (also read other side of this form).

In some instances, the suspect may be issued a citation for an offense at the scene and not taken to jail. In any case, the victim must realize that if it is dangerous to remain at home, one should leave and go to a safe place. Police will assist you as much as possible to find or transport you to a safe place. A victim of domestic violence or sexual assault may ask the District Attorney to file a criminal complaint against the attacker. Telephone (911) 911-1111.

EMERGENCY PROTECTIVE COURT ORDERS

If police on the scene of domestic violence reasonably believe that physical or serious emotional harm has occurred, is threatened or is imminent, they may contact a judicial officer by telephone to obtain an emergency protective order (EPO) to protect the life of the adults and minor children involved. This order will only last for a few days to provide time for victims to obtain a more permanent regular restraining order (Temporary Restraining Order – TRO).

TEMPORARY AND REGULAR RESTRAINING COURT ORDERS

You have a right to go to the Superior Court, Anytown Judicial District, 400 Civic Center Plaza, Anytown, CA 91000 and file a petition requesting any of the following orders for relief at no cost: ▸ An order restraining the attacker from abusing the victim and other family members. ▸ An order directing the attacker to leave the household. ▸ An order preventing the attacker from entering the residence, school, business or place of employment of the victim. ▸ An order awarding the victim or the other parent custody of or visitation with a minor child or children. ▸ An order restraining the attacker from molesting or interfering with minor children in the custody of the victim. ▸ An order directing the party not granted custody to pay support of the minor children, if that party has a legal obligation to do so. ▸ An order directing the defendant to make specific debt payments coming due while the order is in effect. ▸ An order directing that either or both parties participate in counseling.

CIVIL SUIT

A victim has the right to file a civil suit for losses suffered as a result of the abuse, including medical expenses, loss of earnings, expenses for injuries sustained, damage to property, other related expenses incurred by the victim and any agency that shelters the victim.

VICTIM SHELTER – SAFE HOUSES – SUPPORT GROUPS – OUTREACH PROGRAMS

For further information about availability of shelters and other services in the community:

▸ House of Ruth – 24-Hour Hotline – 911-911-1111
▸ Y.W.C.A. Wings - 24-Hour Hotline – 911-911-1111

▸ National Domestic Violence Hotline – 1-911-911-1111
▸ Info Line for Los Angeles County – 911-911-1111
▸ Domestic Violence Hotline – 1-911-911-1111

DOMESTIC VIOLENCE RAPE AND SEXUAL ASSAULT VICTIM INFORMATION

Sexual assault by a person who is known to the victim, including sexual assault by a person who is the spouse of the victim, is a crime. Sexual assaults are serious crimes. These crimes do not just happen between strangers. Get to a safe place. Call – 911 – immediately for police and paramedics. Call a friend or family member you trust. Even if you do not wish to prosecute, police need information you possess which may help apprehend the suspect. If the assault just occurred, do not shower, bathe, douche, change wash or destroy clothing worn during the assault or straighten up the area. Go to a hospital for treatment and an examination. You can go on your own or the police can arrange transportation.

RAPE AND SEXUAL ASSAULT VICTIM COUNSELING CENTERS

▸ L.A. Rape and Battering Hotline – 911-911-1111

▸ Project Sister Rape Crisis Center 24-Hours Hotline, Anytown, CA – 911-911-1111

▸ C.P.A.F. (Asian) Rape & Battering Hotline (many Asian & Pacific languages available) 1-911-911-1111 or 911-911-1111

DOMESTIC VIOLENCE RELATED CHILD ABUSE

To report in progress or just occurred child abuse and neglect, **phone – 911 -**. To report past abuse, phone the police department or Anytown County Department of Children & Family Services Hotline – 1-911-911-1111

NOTICE TO VICTIMS AND PERSONS WHO SUFFER FINANCIAL AND CERTAIN OTHER LOSSES AS A RESULT OF VIOLENT CRIMES AND SPECIFIED ACTS

A program has been established by the State of Any State to provide aid to innocent persons who suffer loss of money due to injury or death caused by people committing violent crimes and specified acts. You may be eligible for this assistance. If you have been the victim of a crime that meets the required definition, you or others may be eligible to receive payment from the Any State Restitution Fund for losses directly resulting from the crime. To learn about eligibility and receive an application, call or contact:

VICTIMS OF CRIME PROGRAM
Any State Victim Compensation & Government Claims Board
P.O. Box 9111, Anytown, CA 91111-1111
Telephone (911) 911-1111
Victims of Crime Website: www.any.ca.gov

VICTIM – WITNESS ASSISTANCE PROGRAM
Anytown County District Attorney's Office
400 Civic Center Plaza, Anytown, CA 91111
Telephone (911) 911-1111 / 911-1111

IMPORTANT NOTICE: Except under unusual circumstances, you have up to one year from the date of the crime to file your claim.

- Side 2 -   APD

DOMESTIC VIOLENCE
VICTIM CONFIDENTIALITY
FORM

(SIDE ONE & SIDE TWO ARE
ON THE NEXT TWO PAGES)

SAMPLE DV HANDOUT

DR #_____

ANYTOWN POLICE DEPARTMENT
VICTIM CONFIDENTIALITY REQUEST

If the victim of a below listed crime(s) elects confidentiality (or the victim's parent or guardian request confidentiality if the victim is a minor) their name, address, business address, school and telephone numbers will not be disclosed to anyone except as provided by law. When confidentiality is elected, sections 293 of the Penal Code and 6254(f)(2)(3) of the Government Code require the omission of such victim information from police records that are made public record. When confidentiality is elected, the victim's personal data will be recorded on this form by the reporting officer. Such victim's name, address and phone numbers will not be released to the public. Victim information will only be released as authorized by law. (Reporting officer – see instructions for completing this form on side 2).

Officer - check all sections that apply. This is a victim of:

☐ 220 PC	☐ 261 PC	☐ 261.5 PC	☐ 262 PC	☐ 264 PC	☐ 264.1 PC	☐ 265 PC	☐ 266 PC
☐ 266 a PC	☐ 266b PC	☐ 266c PC	☐ 266e PC	☐ 266f PC	☐ 266j PC	☐ 267 PC	☐ 269 PC
☐ 273a PC	☐ 273dPC	☐ 273.5 PC	☐ 285 PC	☐ 286 PC	☐ 288 PC	☐ 288a PC	☐ 288.2 PC

☐ 288.3 PC (as added by Chapter 337 of the Statutes of 2006 and/ or as added by Section 6 of Proposition 83 of the November 7, 2006, statewide general election)   ☐ 288.5 PC

☐ 288.7 PC	☐ 289 PC	☐ 422.6 PC	☐ 422.7 PC	☐ 422.75 PC	☐ 646.9 PC	☐ 647.6 PC

The victim was advised their name would be a matter of public record unless confidentiality is requested. The victim:

☐ **REQUESTED CONFIDENTIALITY**   ☐ **DECLINED CONFIDENTIALITY**

The victim requests contact by a victim advocate for information about victim/children's services: ☐Yes   ☐No

Victim's Last Name:	First Name		Middle Name		Sex	Race	Date of Birth
Residence Address		City		State/ Zip	If Victim is a MINOR - Name of Parent		
Home Phone	Cell Phone		Pager #		Other contact #		
Business/School	Address		City/ State/ Zip		Bus. Phone		
Name of Relative or Friend (where victim may get messages)		Address of Relative/Friend			Relative or Friend's Phone #		

X_____

Victim's Signature (or ** see below)   **Date**   **Officer's Signature**

If victim is a minor under the age of 18 years old, obtain the signature of a parent, guardian, Children's Social Worker, or order of a Judicial Officer

---

AUTHORIZATION FOR THE RELEASE OF MEDICAL INFORMATION AND / OR RECORDS

Having been advised of my right to refuse, I hereby consent and authorize Anytown Local Hospital Medical Center, My Town Community Hospital or other listed Health Care Provider _____
and/or Dental Care Provider _____ to release to any official of the Anytown Police Department or the Anytown County District Attorney's Office, any of the medical/dental records requested to assist in the investigation of an incident that was reported to law enforcement. I also hereby relieve your facility, or others, from any and all civil and/or criminal liability which might result from the disclosure of the information requested. A photocopy of this authorization shall be as valid as the original. I understand that I am entitled to receive a copy of this authorization.

Patient's Name (Please Print)	D.O.B.	Identification – DL – Other ID #	Date of Treatment

X_____

Signature of Patient (or parent/guardian if patient is a minor) Authorizing Release of Records   Date

GIVE RECORDS TO OFFICIAL IN PERSON OR MAIL TO: ANYTOWN POLICE DEPARTMENT 2009 THIRD ST, ANYTOWN, CA 90000

THIS IS A CONTROLLED DOCUMENT – THE ORIGINAL IS TO BE RETAINED AT THE ANYTOWN POLICE DEPARTMENT

- SIDE 1 -   (2008)

59

INSTRUCTIONS FOR THE REPORTING OFFICER TO COMPLETE
THIS VICTIM CONFIDENTIALITY REQUEST FORM

I. **An Anytown Police Officer taking a report of any crime(s) listed on the reverse side of this form:**

   A. Shall inform the victim (or parent, legal guardian or assigned social worker if victim is a minor) that their name and address will become a matter of public record unless he or she request that it not become a matter of public record pursuant to Penal Code Section 293 and Government Code 6254(f)(2).

   B. Shall indicate in the report that the alleged victim has been property informed and shall memorialize his or her response and this form is that report.
      1. The officer shall mark the box indicating whether the victim requests or declines confidentiality.

   C. Shall, after checking the appropriate response made by the victim, request the victim (or responsible person above if victim is a minor) to sign the confidentiality form where indicated.
      1. If the victim (or responsible party) refuses or fails to sign, the officer shall write "refused" or "failed to sign in the victim's signature area.
      2. After the victim (or responsible party) signs or refuses/fails to sign, the office shall date and sign in the appropriate area.

   D. Shall, if the victim (or responsible party) declines to make a choice as to whether or not to request or decline confidentiality, **not** mark either confidentiality box and shall write "refused to comply" in the victim's signature area.
      1. **In any case**, when completing an investigation requiring this form, the officer shall sign and date the form.

II. **Authorization for the release of medical information section of this form.**

   A. When ever an officer completes a report for any crime(s) listed on the reverse side of this form, he/she shall complete this section of the form **whether or not** the victim receives medical treatment. In many instances, the victim may seek medical/dental care at a later date and it may be difficult for officers to re-contact the victim.

      1. Circle or enter the appropriate medical hospital or dental office name where provided.
      2. Make every effort to obtain the victim's/ patient's identification – DL – or other ID # and enter same.
      3. **Print** victim's/patient's name, DOB, and date of treatment (if unknown, otherwise, leave blank).
      4. Request victim (or parent/ guardian if victim is a minor) to sign the form where indicated.
      5. If the victim (or parent/ guardian if victim is a minor) refuses or fails to sign, the officer shall write "refused" or "failed to sign" in the victim's/ patient's signature area.
      6. After the victim/patient signs, refuses/fails to sign, the officer shall date and sign in the appropriate area.

III. **Every Anytown Police Officer completing an investigation/report involving any victim of a crime listed on the reverse side of this form shall complete this form as thoroughly and accurately as possible.**

IV. **This completed form shall be forwarded to a supervisor along with other required reports.**

SAMPLE DV HANDOUT

- SIDE 2 -

(2008)

60

PEACE OFFICER'S VERBAL
SERVICE OF A
RESTRAINING/
PROTECTIVE ORDER UPON
A RESTRAINED PARTY
FORM

(SIDE ONE & SIDE TWO ARE
ON THE NEXT TWO PAGES)

ANYTOWN PEACE OFFICER'S VERBAL SERVICE OF A RESTRAINING ORDER OR PROTECTIVE ORDER UPON A RESTRAINED PERSON

DR #

VERBAL SERVICE: A Peace Officer verbally notifies the restrained person that a Domestic Violence Restraining Order, Protective Order or Harassment Restraining Order has been issued against him or her by a Court in this State or another State and advises that person of the terms of the order and directs that person to go to the court to obtain a copy of the order. **THIS IS A VALID VERBAL PROOF OF SERVICE OF THE COURT ORDER UPON THE RESTRAINED PARTY**

DATE OF SERVICE_____ TIME_____ R. D. _____ LOCATION/ ADD. OF SERVICE:_____
CITY:_____ STATE:____ ZIP:_____ REASON FOR POLICE CONTACT WITH THIS PERSON – _____
_____ _____ RELATED CITATION # (IF ANY) _____ RELATED DR # (IF ANY) _____

OFFICER – YOU MUST COMPLETE THE NECESSARY INFORMATION BELOW AND THEN READ ALL INFORMATION IN THIS BOX ALOUD TO THE RESTRAINED PARTY, IF NECESSARY, USE A TRANSLATOR. IF POSSIBLE, HAVE A WITNESSING EMPLOYEE -

PROTECTED PERSON(S) NAME(S):_____
TERMS OF ORDER TOLD TO RESTRAINED PERSON: □ Stay away at least _____ yards from each person I just named. □ Stay away at least _____ yards from the following addresses /places____ _____
□ Move out immediately from _____ □ Special orders _____
□ You must <u>not</u> contact, molest, harass, attack, strike, threaten, sexually assault, batter, telephone, send any messages to, follow, stalk, destroy any personal property, or disturb the peace of any protected person I just named.
□ (Name) _____ is given temporary care and control of the following minor children (name & ages) _____
□ (Name) _____ is given custody of the following children (name &ages) _____
▶ GET A COPY OF ORDER AT THIS ISSUING COURT: _____COURT CASE # _____JUDGE _____
▶ DATE COURT ORDER WAS ISSUED _____ - DATE COURT ORDER EXPIRES _____

TO THE RESTRAINED PARTY – PERSONS SUBJECT TO A RESTRAINING ORDER ARE PROHIBITED FROM OWNING, POSSESSING, PURCHASING, RECEIVING, OR ATTEMPTING TO PUCHASE OR RECEIVE A FIREARM AS LONG AS THIS ORDER IS IN EFFECT – SEE PENAL CODE SECTION 12021(g) – IT IS A CRIME AND YOU WILL BE ARRESTED IF YOU VIOLATE THIS FIREARM PROHIBITION.

* □ ADDITIONALLY, (IF COURT ORDERED)- [OFFICER CHECK WITH DISPATCER/ DVROS FOR SPECIFICS] – YOU ARE ORDERED BY THE COURT TO RELINQUISH ANY FIREARM(S) IN YOUR IMMEDIATE POSSESSION OR CONTROL OR SUBJECT TO YOUR IMMEDIATE POSSESSION OR CONTROL TO A LAW ENFORCEMENT OFFICER – YOU MUST SURRENDER THE FIREARM(S) IMMEDIATELY (IF YOU HAVE IT). IF YOU DO NOT POSSESS OR CONTROL THE FIREARM(S) AT THIS MOMENT, YOU HAVE 24 HOURS TO SURRENDER THE FIREARM(S) IN A SAFE MANNER TO A LAW ENFORCEMENT OFFICER OR BY SELLING THE FIREARM(S) TO A LICENSED GUN DEALER AS SPECIFIED IN 12071 OF THE CALIFORNIA PENAL CODE – AFTER SURRENDERING OR SELLING THE FIREARM(S) YOU HAVE [OFFICER CHECK ONE-SEE ORDER] – □ 48 HOURS OR □ 72 HOURS – , AFTER BEING SERVED WITH THIS NOTICE, TO FILE A RECEIPT WITH THE COURT SHOWING THE FIREARM(S) WAS SURRENDERED TO LAW ENFORCEMENT OR SOLD TO A LICENSED GUN DEALER.

RESTRAINED PERSON BEING SERVED:

▶
| Name: Last | First | Middle | Maiden/ Other Name | Bus. Phone No | Home Phone No. |

▶

| Residence: Address | | Apt., Sp., Rm. No. | City | State | Zip |

DOB	Age	Race	Sex	Ht.	Wt.	Hair	Eyes	SS#	DL#	State
Restrained Party's Vehicle	Year		Make		Model		Style		License	State	Color

I acknowledge VERBAL service of a Domestic Violence Restraining Order, Protective Order or Harassment Restraining Order in accordance with Section 6383 (and other sections) of the California Family Code, Penal Code and Federal Law. I understand that verbal service is sufficient notice to prohibit the owning, possessing, purchasing, receiving, or attempting to purchase or receive a firearm, as long as this order is in effect (6389 Family Code & 12021(g) Penal Code). I have been told to relinquish any firearms and file a receipt with the court. I have been told to obtain an official copy of this order containing the full terms and conditions from the issuing court above.

X_____ _____
    Signature of person served   *Date*

▶ **The above person was served by:**	Indicate if translator was used (Person's Name-Agency-Other)
X_____ *Signature of Officer* *Serial #* *Date*	_____ Note any related comments made by restrained person (was he aware of court order, etc.)_____

- Side 1 -

ANYTOWN POLICE DEPARTMENT
VERBAL SERVICE OF A RESTRAINING ORDER – INSTRUCTIONS FOR POLICE PERSONNEL

VERBAL SERVICE OF A DOMESTIC VIOLENCE RESTRAINING ORDER, PROTECTIVE ORDER OR HARASSMENT RESTRAINING ORDER ISSUED BY THIS STATE, OTHER STATE, COMMONWEALTH, TERRITORY, INSULAR POSSESSION SUBJECT TO JURISDICTION OF THE UNITED STATES, MILITARY TRIBUNAL OR TRIBE.

NOTE: VERBAL NOTICE OF A PROTECTIVE OR RESTRAINING ORDER GIVEN BY A PEACE OFFICER IS VALID SERVICE TO MEET THE REQUIREMENTS FOR ARREST FOR VIOLATION OF SUCH ORDER UNDER 273.6 P.C. AND 136.2 P.C. [136.2 P.C. IS A PENAL CODE AUTHORITY WHICH ALSO INCLUDES CHARGES OF 166 (a)(4), (c)(1) AND (c)(4)]. *DO NOT USE THIS FORM TO RECORD SERVICE OF AN ACTUAL COPY OF THE ORDER UPON A RESTRAINED PARTY. THIS FORM IS FOR VERBAL SERVICE ONLY.*

This form updates the status of the order in the DOJ DVROS computer system to that of the restrained party having been served proper notice of the domestic violence restraining order or other order described above.

This form and notice may be used if this agency (or any other agency that enters court orders into the DOJ DVROS system) holds the order. A peace officer may verbally serve proper notice upon any person who is in custody or who is lawfully contacted (subject check, traffic stop, reporting party, etc.) that he or she is the restrained party of a restraining, protective or civil harassment court order

If an Anytown Police Officer confirms such order is listed in the DOJ DVROS computer system, and determines that the restrained party has not been served, he or she shall use the reverse side of this form to document and complete proper service.

Verbal notice from a peace officer to a restrained party that a court order against him or her exist and informing that person of the contents of the order (restrained actions) and advising the person to go to the appropriate court to obtain a copy of the order constitutes proper notice to the restrained party [F.C. 6224, 6381 and 6383 - P.C. 836(c)(2)].

** INSTRUCTIONS FOR THE PEACE OFFICER **

1. An Anytown Peace Officer comes in lawful contact with a person.
2. An Anytown Peace Officer determines there is a proper court order against the person by locating such order in the DOJ DVROS computer system AND determines proper notice needs to be served.
3. An Anytown Police Officer **shall verbally notify such person of the specific terms of the order** and advise the person to go to the appropriate court to obtain a copy of the order. (Obtain specific orders from communications). Only mark and advise the party of the firearm relinquishment if directed by the court order. Check with the communications officer. Do not guess.
4. The above officer fully completes the reverse side of this form and requests the person verbally served to sign the form. If the person refuses, note "REFUSED" in that signature location. It is not a crime for a person to refuse to sign this notice. It is a request only.
5. The above officer signs, dates and forwards the completed form with a DR number to An Anytown PD Communications Officer along with any related reports. **A SUPP DR number should be used if the order is already on file at the A.P.D. and has an existing DR number. If Anytown PD has the hard copy of the order, it is best to serve the restrained party with an actual copy of the order on file, whenever possible. However, verbal service is sufficient notice.**
6. Complete a "WITNESS PAGE" *only* if there are non-departmental civilians, translators or outside agency officials involved as witnesses, etc.

** INSTRUCTIONS FOR THE COMMUNICATIONS OFFICER **

1. Update the DOJ DVROS entry into the computer system and indicate verbal service was made.
2. With an Anytown PD DVROS court order, update the system indicating what type of service was made and attach this form and updated print out as a supp-report to the original order.
3. With an outside agency DOJ DVROS court order, update the system indicating what type of service was made **and** mail or FAX a copy of this form (both sides) to the agency that made the DVROS entry.
4. Fully complete, sign and date the below area of this form and obtain another Comm. Ofc's verification stamp or signature and date prior to forwarding / faxing or mailing this form.
5. **Obtain the on duty Watch Commander's approval at the below area of this form when complete and processed.**
6. The form **and** updated DVROS system print out is a completed DR and is processed through records as usual.

:: BELOW IS FOR USE BY COMMUNICATIONS OFFICERS AND SUPERVISORS ONLY ::

MODIFY ORIGINAL ENTRY OF AN ANYTOWN POLICE DEPARTMENT DVROS: FCN # _____

MODIFY ENTRY OF OTHER POLICE AGENCY'S DVROS - ORDER SERVED (VERBAL SERVICE) BY ANYTOWN P. D. _____

OTHER AGENCY NAME	OTHER AGENCY CASE #	FCN #

COM -OFC. SHALL SEND A COPY OF THIS FORM (BOTH SIDES) OF ANOTHER AGENCY'S DVROS SERVICE TO THAT AGENCY – METHOD OF NOTIFICATION → [] MAILED   [] FAXED

COMMUNICATIONS OFFICER(S) PROCESSING _____ __ _____ -- DATE _____
                                     Name   Name

WATCH COMMANDER APPROVAL_____ – DATE _____

- Side 2 -   FORM # (2008)

XIX. DOMESTIC VIOLENCE DOMINANT AGGRESSOR "DECISION TREE"

This DV dominant aggressor "Decision Tree" is provided by permission and courtesy of the Police Chiefs' Association of Santa Clara County's "Domestic Violence Protocol for Law Enforcement" – 2007 – by permission of Chair, Chief Bruce Cumming, Morgan Hill Police Department (per Commander David Swing, Morgan Hill P.D.)

DOMINANT AGGRESSOR "DECISION TREE"

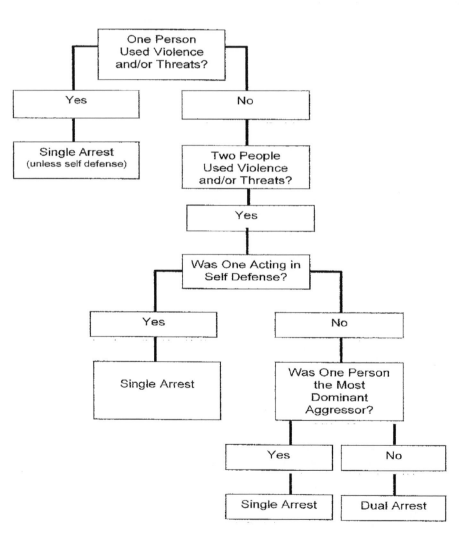

XX. DOMESTIC VIOLENCE FLOW CHART

This DV flow chart is provided by permission and courtesy of the Police Chiefs' Association of Santa Clara County's "Domestic Violence Protocol for Law Enforcement" – 2007 – by permission of Chair, Chief Bruce Cumming, Morgan Hill Police Department (per Commander David Swing, Morgan Hill P.D.)

DOMESTIC VIOLENCE FLOW CHART

Processes charted below apply to both adult <u>and</u> juvenile cases.

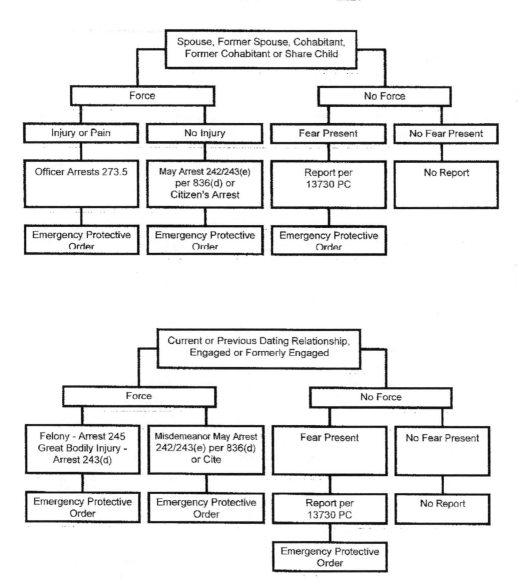

XXI. EIGHT (8) STEPS TO REMMEMBER FOR DOMESTIC VIOLENCE RESPONSE

GET A NEW ATTITUDE !!

1. **Stay alive!** You can't help anyone (including you partner) if you are seriously injured or dead. Due to handling hundreds of DV calls in your career, it is very easy to become complacent without even noticing it. Critique yourself, your partner; look for ways to improve officer safety. These are very dangerous calls. Just because you got through the first 100 calls, doesn't mean you will survive the 101st.

2. **Be willing to change!** If you are stagnant, then you are stuck in the mud. Improve yourself; your handling of DV calls; learn new methods; get training; details . . . details . . . details.

3. **Expect uncooperative or angry victims and witnesses . . . it is part of the phenomenon of domestic violence.** That should not surprise you. If that angers or discourages you then you are not prepared to handle DV calls (get a new attitude & fall back to step # 2, above).

4. **Care about victims and children of DV relationships,** even if they don't seem to care about themselves . . . because no one else will.

5. **Place minor children into protective custody & remove them from the home** when both parents are violent or aggressive towards the children or they are unable or unwilling to provide a safe environment for the children (that includes one parent failing to remove the abuser parent from the children via lawful means). Yeah, I know it takes a lot of your time and it is a pain in the rump, but do it any way – remember your "Law Enforcement Officer's Code of Ethics", which states in part, "my fundamental duty is to serve mankind; to safeguard lives and property; to protect the innocent against deception, the weak against oppression or intimidation, and the peaceful against violence or disorder".

6. **Obtain emergency protective orders (EPO's) whenever possible!** Not only when someone asks or pleads for one.

7. **Do the most – whatever is possible – be proactive!** That includes completing a good investigation & report. Don't do the minimum, or the least, or what you must do to "just get out of the call".

8. **Work as a team,** with: officers, detectives, district attorneys, victims, victim services, witnesses, probation, etc.

XXII. THE PEACE OFFICER'S "BIG PICTURE" DUTY

There is no doubt that an improved peace officer response to domestic violence is the key goal of this book. That said, peace officers have additional responsibilities to continue general law enforcement duties in a variety of other areas. Officers should always keep a keen eye and ear open during any law enforcement contact so that they become aware of any dangers or other criminal activity that may accompany a domestic violence call.

Officers should be aware that circumstances may change at any given moment during the investigation of the domestic violence incident. The parties involved may change from victim to suspect, suspect to victim or both becoming suspects in another crime, possibly unrelated to the original incident.

Officers are cautioned to never: "boot strap" circumstances, make false statements in reports, conduct searches they know are illegal, make knowingly false arrests, "create" emergency situations to advance a search or seizure and never, never, never commit perjury.

However, peace officers should not close their eyes to criminal activity which occurs before them. Officers should expand investigations, searches and probable cause to arrest when done so in a lawful manner. The trained and motivated proactive peace officer may use many skills to expand the opportunities in a proper police investigation.

Scenario examples of changing or unusual circumstances:

- Peace officers at the scene of domestic violence between husband and wife ask the victim female if there are any weapons in the home to carry out the intent of PC 12028.5 (weapons seizure during domestic violence incidents). The wife in her upset state quickly advises that the husband keeps a loaded revolver under their bed and gives the officer consent to seize and remove it for her protection.

  o *The officer looks under the bed and, in addition to the gun, sees in plain sight a sizeable amount of methamphetamine, along with packaging materials and scales for the sales of narcotics. Further investigation reveals both husband and wife are jointly selling illegal narcotics and both are arrested for a felony crime.*

- A peace officer responds to a domestic violence case between a married couple at their home that is determined to be a misdemeanor battery [PC 243 (a)] that just occurred. The officer is aware that the suspect wife has been arrested many times for felony narcotic violations. Several of those arrests occurred at that same address. The victim husband does not want an arrest or an EPO. Even though this is a misdemeanor violation not committed in the officer's presence, the officer knows PC 836 (d) allows the arrest of this battery suspect, with probable cause, in this situation.

  o *Even though the victim spouse does not want the arrest to be made, the officer makes the misdemeanor arrest of the suspect wife under the authority of PC 836 (d).*

- The suspect is transported to the PD jail where she is searched and heroin, marijuana and narcotic sales notations are found in her possession.

- Officers obtain a search warrant for the suspect's home based upon the probable cause that drug possession and drug sales are taking place at the residence.

- Officers respond to the suspect's home, conduct the warrant search and find more narcotics, evidence of drug sales, money, illegal weapons and drug paraphernalia. The officers conduct a further investigation at the scene and both husband and wife are determined to be in violation of serious felony crimes and are arrested.

- A peace officer makes a routine traffic stop for excessive speed and a brake light not functioning. The officer contacts the male driver and female passenger. The driver is the owner of the vehicle. The officer makes a standard warrant check over the police radio while writing the traffic citation for the violation. Dispatch advises that the driver has no wants or warrants but he is the restrained party in a valid emergency protective order (EPO) that has been served upon him. The order was issued and served just the previous day. The protected party is a female by the name of Valerie Victim, who was the restrained party's girlfriend. The restrained party is not to contact or be within 100 yards of the protected female for any reason. The officer contacts the couple and she admits she is the protected party and he confirms he is the restrained party. She adds that they "made up and got back together". They said they did not go back to court to have the restraining order terminated. Both parties said they did not want any arrest to be made.

  - The officer makes the arrest of the restrained party per PC 13701 (b) and PC 836 (c)(1).

  - The officer knows, per PC 13710 (b), that the terms and conditions of the protection order remain enforceable, notwithstanding the acts of the parties, and may be changed only by order of the court. In other words, the court is ordering the officer to make the arrest even if the parties do not want such an arrest to be made.

  - The officer knows that Family Code (FC) 6272 (a) requires that a law enforcement officer shall use every reasonable means to enforce an emergency protective order, and that FC 6272 (b) and FC 6383 (h) states that a law enforcement officer who acts in good faith to enforce an emergency protective order, protective order or restraining order is not civilly or criminally liable.

  - After making the "custodial arrest" of the driver, the officer searches the car and finds a loaded revolver under the driver's seat next to a purse with a driver's license and credit card in the name of another female. The officer conducts and investigation and discovers the I.D. belonged to another "girlfriend" of the restrained party and the gun was used to murder that woman the night before in a neighboring city. The driver is charged with murder.

- A peace officer responds to a home on a domestic violence call between a man and a woman who live together like husband and wife (common-law type relationship). Officers have been there before on a number of domestic violence calls. Several of those past calls have resulted in the man being arrested for battery upon this same woman. He has one past conviction of PC 243 battery upon this female, but he is no longer on probation. The couple now has a 9-month-old child living in the home. On this call, the man came home upset about issues at work. He is slamming his fists into the walls of their home, yelling and cursing, has been drinking beer but is not drunk, is throwing books and objects inside the home, and is blaming his common-law wife for all their problems. The wife says she is afraid of him and feels threatened but no crime has been committed yet. She refuses to request an Emergency Protective Order (EPO) and specifically tells the officer she does not want such an order.

o The officer knows that no actual crime has occurred, so he or she can not arrest the male party. However, the officer knows of the repeated violence and anger displayed by the man resulting in several previous arrests for him battering this same woman. He knows the man has one previous conviction for PC 243 on this same common-law wife. There is now a small baby present in the home where this man is currently displaying anger and aggressive out of control behavior. The woman says she is fearful of the man and feels threatened. However, she refuses to request an EPO and does not want the protective order.

o Based upon the totality of the circumstances, the officer feels there are reasonable grounds to believe the common-law wife and their child, are in immediate and present danger of domestic violence [as described in FC 6203 (c) and 6250 (a) & (b)] based upon: the fact that several past calls have resulted in the same man being arrested for battery upon this same woman, with one arrest resulting in his conviction for PC 243; the man is upset, slamming his fists into the walls of their home, yelling and cursing, has been drinking beer, is throwing books and objects inside the home and blames his common-law wife for all their problems; thus, the man is currently displaying anger and aggressive out of control behavior which creates an immediate threat of abuse towards the wife and child.

o The officer requests an EPO from the on-call judicial officer who issues a protective order. The officer serves the man at the location and orders him to leave immediately. The restrained man either:

1. Immediately obeys the order and leaves the location with no arrest involved, **or**

2. He refuses to leave and is arrested for violating the EPO. The fact that the common-law wife did not want the EPO or even if she insisted he not be arrested would have no bearing on the validity of the EPO or the arrest for violating the order. Further, the totality of the circumstances would lead a reasonable officer to believe that the threat would continue or resume and that the safety of persons would be imminently endangered by the release. In specific, a reasonable officer would believe the female would let the abuser back in the home if he were to be O.R. released. Therefore, per PC 853.6 (a) the abuser should remain in jail and not be O.R. released.

- A peace officer responds to a domestic violence incident between a married couple at their home. They have a 12-year-old daughter who is currently visiting at a neighbor's house. Police contact them on their back patio. The man is bleeding from the right ear and a 3-foot long stick, with blood on it, is on the patio nearby. The wife is crying and readily admits she hit her husband after a verbal argument. She says her husband did not attack, hit or injure her. There are no visible injuries on her. The husband says little, other than he did not assault his wife. Paramedics arrive and state the man needs several stitches to his ear and transport him to the hospital. The wife is arrested for PC 273.5 and 245 ADW and taken to jail. The neighbors continue to watch the couple's child at the parents' request.

o At the police station, the wife breaks down and says that the reason she lost control and struck her husband was because she had just found out he had been sexually molesting their 12-year-old daughter. She says the daughter broke down earlier that day and described how "daddy" had her orally copulate him and that he had sodomized and had sexual intercourse with her several times over the last few months. When the wife confronted her husband with the claim he confessed that he did have those sexual relations with the daughter.

- The police then interviewed the daughter and she gave very clear and convincing statements confirming the crimes outlined by the mother. The police also had the child examined at the hospital and those medical findings confirmed evidence of sexual intercourse and sodomy.

- The husband was contacted at the hospital at the time of his release. He made several pre-arrest admissions stating he did have sexual intercourse and sodomy with his daughter. He was arrested at that time and later confessed after waiving his rights. He was charged with several serious felony sex crimes.

XXIII.   A FINAL WORD

Properly enforcing domestic violence laws to protect victims is not the only responsibility of the law enforcement officer. But it certainly is one of the top priorities of any well trained professional peace officer. Always remember that in many domestic violence cases that have turned deadly, often police had prior domestic violence contacts with the same parties. Unfortunately, in some cases, the failure of law enforcement to _properly_ act contributed to deadly consequences later. Repeated domestic violence committed by an abuser who faces little or no formal consequences, emboldens that criminal to commit future, and often more vicious, attacks upon the same victim.

Remember to _follow_ the *"Law Enforcement Officer's Code of Ethics".* It's not just words. It's real . . . and part of you . . . it speaks to you and about you and it acts as a moral guidance system that propels you to do the right thing. *So now it is time . . . get up and go do what is right.*

Domestic Violence Response – A Guide for California Peace Officers is directed specifically at the first responder – the cop on the street. There is much to consider when dealing with the domestic violence victim ... the abuser ... the children. Peace officers must ask themselves, "Do I really know what I must do?" This book provides:

- *Practical tools officers can use – today*
- *A quick reference guide of domestic violence crimes*
- *Samples of useful forms for domestic violence investigations*
- *An in-depth review of domestic violence crimes and authorities*
- *Tips to help the individual officer with curtailing domestic violence*
- *Information and procedures to increase service of court restraining orders*
- *Motivation for officers to carry out their duties to protect victims and themselves*

What people are saying about "Domestic Violence Response – A Guide for California Peace Officers" –

"This book clarifies why it is critical for every officer and police agency throughout California to be armed with the most updated materials related to domestic violence in order to enhance both public and officer safety."

Steven M. Barba – Detective-II, Los Angeles Police Department-Retired

"This book that Randy Latham has authored, regarding domestic violence, is the most user friendly and comprehensive document for any officer or agency to have in their library. Latham's attention to detail assures proper and legal handling of domestic violence cases while promoting officers to do what is required of them."

Chuck Ochoa – MSLM (Master of Science in Leadership and Management), Police Department Support Services Supervisor, Police Academy Instructor

"Randy's book, *Domestic Violence Response – A Guide for California Peace Officers*, provides an excellent resource for field personnel as well as investigators and will definitely assist law enforcement agencies in their response to incidents of domestic violence."

Scott Pickwith – Chief of Police, La Verne Police Department

authorHOUSE®

ISBN 978-1-4389-5081-5

90000

9 781438 950815